VITAL
SIGNS
of
FAITH

VITAL
SIGNS
of
FAITH

Finding Health
in Your
Spiritual Life

KATE MOOREHEAD CARROLL

FORWARD MOVEMENT
CINCINNATI, OHIO

Library of Congress Control Number: 2022938514

Scripture quotations are from the New Revised Standard Version of the Bible, copyright ©1989 the National Council of the Churches of Christ in the United States of America.

Psalm quotations are from the Book of Common Prayer.

"Breathing Underwater" by Carol Bialock, RSCJ appears in *Coral Castles* (Fernwood Press), copyright 2019. Used by permission.

#2632

ISBN: 978-0-880-28503-2

© 2022 Forward Movement

www.forwardmovement.org

This book is dedicated to
Dr. Chris Carroll, my husband,
who has taught me about
health of body, mind, and spirit.

Table of Contents

Preface

I walked into my parents' bedroom one evening to tell them that I felt God calling me to become a priest. As former Hindus turned Episcopalians, they still slept on a mattress on the floor as the Hindus did. I was 19 years old.

I have a terrible long-term memory, but I remember this moment as if it were yesterday.

I was gazing at their dresser. A strange vision came into my mind. I pictured standing on a rock in a vast body of water. As the tide began to rise, I was going to have to jump from rock to rock to survive. Somehow, instinctively, I understood that I would be able to serve in these beautiful churches, but I would have to jump from one to the other as the rising tide of secularism began to sweep people away. I would have time to be a priest as the church was gently submerging and becoming something entirely new. I would be running out of time.

As a child, I made up a game called "The Ship Game." It was similar in nature to my vision. My friends and I pretended that we were on a ship and the water was rising. We could jump to a small island or a rock from our boat and then back again. We put pillows all over the floor and leaped from one to the other. But if we touched the water, we died. Sometimes we upgraded the water to lava. It was fun.

As a Gen-X child whose parents raised me in the shadow of the Cold War and who built a bomb shelter in their basement, it's no wonder I thought that life as I knew it might end. I think I pretended to jump from pillow to pillow in my living room to express the anxiety that lived inside me. The world was changing rapidly. Could I keep up with the change? How would people and institutions change? As I grew and discerned a call to the priesthood, the question haunted me: in the face of this changing world, would the church adapt and grow?

We do not understand the magnitude of the historic transition that consumes us. The arrival of technology and the ability to communicate across the planet in seconds is altering our minds. Our brains are in a period of adjustment that causes great anxiety, depression, and a constant state of restlessness. We are evolving—as the waters rise above our heads, our very nature is changing. We will soon be submerged into a new kind of interconnected world where technology integrates into every aspect of our lives. We will be living in communion with computers.

Over the course of history, new inventions have changed the landscape of our lives and of our churches. When the printing press was invented around 1436, the church in the Western Hemisphere was altered forever. People began to read the Bible in their own language, and when they read about Jesus walking around as a poor man, they began to wonder why the church was so rich. The resulting Reformation and Counter-Reformation were painful and bloody, but the impetus was genuine and truthful—we had strayed from the way of Jesus.

Today, I am a long way from that young woman who first discerned God's call to ministry. But my vision has held true. As the tide of change rises, I have had to jump from rock to rock, learning and leading congregations into this new way of being. I now serve as dean of a cathedral in Jacksonville, Florida. Sometimes I watch the faces of strangers who walk into the cathedral for the first time. They are struck by the beauty of the sanctuary, the way the light streams the stories of Jesus's life through stained-glass windows, how the music elevates the soul to new heights. They watch as the altar party processes down the aisle in robes and carrying candles, and it is all fascinating. It is art. But many have not grown up in a church tradition, and they don't know the reasoning behind each movement. They don't resonate with the cadence of the ancient words that those of us who grew up in the church have spoken repeatedly, for our entire lives. The service seems long and rather incomprehensible to them. They wonder what it has to do with Jesus. They are drawn to the mystery and pageantry and see the worship and buildings as beautiful and fascinating pieces of art. But they don't attend worship regularly and wonder if this is where they belong. They are without root.

The first Christians huddled together in their homes and shared a meal together. Over the meal, they remembered Jesus and how he gave his life so that they could live eternally. They shared bread and wine and believed that these became his body and blood. This simple act of sharing a meal became so sacred that they eventually built beautiful cathedrals to house that meal, and they composed profound music to express their gratitude. Still, even the height of beauty could not capture its essence. They could not have foreseen how that same beauty would at times become an idol. They could not have foreseen how their simple meal at home could evolve into a ritual whose execution would threaten to become more important than the message itself if they were not diligent and disciplined and very, very careful.

Each year, I look at our budget. We are a lively and thriving cathedral in the core of the city of Jacksonville. People are incredibly faithful and generous, and yet, our facility is so expensive that each year I pray we will have enough money to minister and keep up the maintenance. And in the years to come, will it be enough?

Across the country, smaller churches are closing their doors. Churches across the United States and Europe are sitting empty or becoming museums, restaurants, and apartments. The Episcopal cathedral in Rhode Island is now a museum. We have closed numerous churches in Florida, but we don't talk about it much. I suppose we feel like failures, forgetting that our Lord died for us and maybe we, too, must die in order to live.

As the water rises and the smaller rocks are covered by the tide, I look to the great cathedrals. Will the tide of secularism cover them too? The pandemic has birthed virtual worship and online communities. Are they to last into the future?

There is a beautiful poem written by Carol Bialock, RSCJ:

> I built my house by the sea.
> Not on the sands, mind you;
> Not on the shifting sand.
> And I built it of rock.
> A strong house
> by a strong sea.
> And we got well acquainted, the sea and I.
> Good neighbors.
> Not that we spoke much.
> We met in silences.
> Respectful, keeping our distance,
> but looking our thoughts across the fence of sand.
> Always, the fence of sand our barrier,
> always, the sand between.
> And then one day,
> —and I still don't know how it happened—
> the sea came.
> Without warning.
> Without welcome, even.
> Not sudden and swift, but a shifting across the sand
>   like wine,

less like the flow of water than the flow of blood.
Slow, but coming.
Slow, but flowing like an open wound.
And I thought of flight and I thought of drowning
and I thought of death.
And while I thought the sea crept higher, till it
reached my door.
And I knew then, there was neither flight, nor death,
nor drowning.
That when the sea comes calling you stop being
Neighbors
Well acquainted, friendly-at-a-distance, neighbors
And you give your house for a coral castle,
And you learn to breathe underwater.

We are becoming submerged in a new kind of reality, one in which technology shapes our minds. But we can learn to breathe underwater. The breath of God, the Holy Spirit, will find us amidst the chaos of this new age. We will, once more, be reborn of water and the spirit.

We must find it again—the essence of our life together, the things that keep us alive—and, taking a deep breath, step into the water.

Introduction

Years ago, I went dogsledding with my youngest son in the Yukon. The temperature was 38 below zero. Max, an incredibly strong outdoorsman, kept looking behind to check on me as we rode our dogsleds single file. I think he was afraid that I would fall or, worse, let go of the dogsled, but I held on.

I learned from Max that when the body is very cold, you should focus on the heart. Keep your core warm, he said. Focus on your heart and your breath.

As the waters of secularism rise, I want us Christians to take this simple advice and focus on our vital signs. What is our heartbeat? What do we want to take with us into the new age? What should we leave behind?

I try to get a check-up each year. Each year, my doctor discusses various issues with me. She asks me if I am exercising regularly. How is my diet? She tells me that as a middle-aged woman I need to lift weights because my bones are beginning to decline (she uses much more impressive language like impending osteopenia). She talks about the coming of menopause, checking for breast cancer and other issues. It is a detailed exam, and I am grateful for her thoroughness. I am truly blessed to have medical care.

Why do we not examine our spiritual health with the same intention? I believe it is time for faith leaders to provide our people with ways to measure, nurture, and develop the life of the spirit. Just as we care for our bodies, so we must learn to care for our hearts, minds, and souls. The physical life and the spiritual life are both vital. One influences and impacts the other. Why do we spend time on our bodies alone and not also on our souls?

After 25 years of struggle, my marriage failed. I had to start a new life as a single woman. I had only lived alone for one year after college before marriage. I had never made my own budget, paid my bills, or filed my own taxes. Here I was, the dean of a cathedral, managing a budget of more than $2 million, and I had never run my own household. I felt like a very strange over-aged child. I thought I would be alone for the rest of my life—well, not alone. I would be married to Jesus.

I announced my divorce on Facebook. As a public figure, I thought it best to get the news out there in my own words before people heard through grapevines and phone calls. To my great surprise, my first kiss from high school sent me a message. He, too, was recently divorced. He is a doctor living in Connecticut. We began to talk.

Months later, we arranged to meet in person. It had been 31 years since I had seen him. We fell in love. God amazes me sometimes—well, a lot of times.

So, I found myself in a significant, long-distant relationship with a doctor. He began to speak to me about his work, and it occurred to me how similar we are. Chris looks after the physical health of a person (specifically children as a pediatric intensivist), and I look after the spiritual health of a person. If Chris were walking down a street and found someone lying on the ground unconscious, his first step would be to check the four vital signs.

1. Is the person breathing?
2. Does the person have a pulse?
3. What is their temperature?
4. What is their blood pressure?

From these four basic pieces of information, Chris would then begin to go deeper and try to address whatever ails the person. It is from these simple vital signs that all treatment begins.

Wellness begins with the simple principle of truth-telling. We must look at where we are, describe our spiritual health, and then strive to care for, maintain, and improve that health. We begin to care for ourselves by taking our vital signs.

But what are the vital signs of the spiritual life? There are four vital signs in the physical life, and four gospels (four ways of telling the story of Jesus), so I believe that it is beneficial to speak of four vital signs in the spiritual life as well. These four vital signs happen to all begin with the letter G, so I have come to call them "The Four Gs." The alliteration makes it easier to remember them, and in the age of the sound bite, brevity is important.

The four vital signs are as follows:

1. GOD: *The Breath*

The word for God in Hebrew, *Yahweh*, literally sounds like a breath. It is as if the ancient Hebrews believed that when we breathe, we are saying the name of God. And so, the first vital sign of the spiritual life must focus on the Creator and our relationship with the one who made us.

Do you spend time with God? Do you pray? Do you worship? The time you spend in devotion is the first vital sign of the spiritual life. And yes, this is measurable. You can measure your minutes, seconds, perhaps hours—the time you give to God. You can measure your full and undivided attention, however long you chose to give it to God. Your attention is valuable; just ask the marketers. How much of your undivided attention do you give to God?

2. GIVE: *The Pulse*

Just as oxygen flows to the heart as we breathe, helping the heart to beat, so time spent with God naturally causes the activity of thankful giving. Do you serve God by giving your time in some way? Do you seek justice, feed the hungry, listen to those in need? Do you give money? Is it sacrificial giving? Giving of both time and money can be measured as well, and this measurement is the second vital sign of the spiritual life.

3. GROW: *The Temperature*

Measuring the temperature of a physical body tells the doctor if the person is failing to thrive or battling illness. Healthy temperature is a delicate balance of the right amount of activity for the cells of the body. Temperature is caused by the movement of the cells within the body.

In the spiritual life, a person must learn and grow—must move toward God—to be healthy and alive. Are you learning, reflecting, studying, asking questions? If Christ is alive within you, then your life will be in constant motion. Growth can be measured by engagement. Are you reading scripture and studying your faith tradition? Are you actively learning in your field and in other areas? Are you seeking to become a better person?

Growth is the most difficult vital sign to measure for it is unique to each person. One way to measure growth is simply to measure your engagement with new ideas: books, classes, videos, podcasts. Are you open to learning?

4. GROUP: *The Pressure*

If your heart is working well and the veins and arteries are not clogged or obstructed, then you should have a healthy blood pressure. The pressure needs to be within a specific range, not too high or too low. Taking blood pressure is a way of measuring a body's physical health. Meeting with a group is similar—it is a tool for measuring spiritual health.

To discern God's will in our lives, we must meet regularly to share our lives with others. We cannot follow Christ alone. Remember that Jesus had a group of disciples. He did this to show us how to walk in this way. It is impossible for one person to discern God's will without the help of others. Just as the blood pressure must be a balanced number, so this group of believers must achieve a delicate balance of love, support, and confidentiality. The group cannot have too few people or too many. This spiritual vital sign is often overlooked, but like the others, it is critical for a balanced, healthy spiritual life. And it is easily measured. Are you meeting weekly with your group? Are you listening and praying for each other?

In evaluating these four vital signs of faith, we can measure the practices that will support and nurture our spiritual health, just as we would measure the vital signs of the body. It is time for us to have access to these tools of the spiritual life so that we may care for ourselves and strengthen our relationship with God.

GOD
The Breath

The mysterious name for God in the Hebrew Scriptures is given in answer to a question from Moses. Moses asks God, "If I come to the Israelites and say to them, 'The God of your ancestors has sent me to you,' and they ask me, 'What is his name?' What shall I say to them?" (Exodus 3:13).

And God answers: *I AM WHO I AM* (Exodus 3:14).

The name in Hebrew is *Yahweh*, but we have no idea how it was pronounced at the time. Many Jews to this day do not utter this name for it is considered too powerful, too holy, so they use the Hebrew word *Adonai*, which means Lord.

The word *Yahweh* sounds a lot like our breath. It is two syllables that come into and go out of the lungs with the air. Could God have been indicating to us that every time we breathe, we are saying the name of the one who created us?

The first vital sign of the spiritual life begins with an acknowledgment that God is as close to us as our own breath. We need to get to know the one who made us and who breathes in and through us. We do this by spending time with God in both prayer and worship. To pray is to awaken a relationship that is already there. It is to acknowledge the deepest kind of love that made us and sustains us.

It is the Trinity, the understanding of God as three in one and one in three, that also points us in the direction of breath and of the flow of air in and out of our bodies. In his book, *Trinity: The Soul of Creation*, Richard Rohr describes the Trinity as three buckets on a moving water wheel, similar to those you might see in Europe. As the wheel turns, each bucket dumps the water, then swings back to be refilled. Rohr writes that many of us aren't willing to take such risks because we're not certain that we will be refilled. But that's not the case with the Trinity, each pouring out and refilling one another, an infinite outpouring and infinite inpouring.

God is a pouring out and a returning. The first vital sign of the spirit simply asks us to track how often and for how long we "stand under the flow," as Richard Rohr describes it. How often do you turn your attention to that outpouring of love? Just as air enters our bodies and then leaves, so we must learn to pray by giving and receiving in a dance with God. To pray and worship, to spend time with God: these are the first steps in developing a life of the spirit. We can measure this first vital sign in terms of time. How often and for how long do you give God your attention in either prayer or worship? Measure the time as you would measure the breath in and out of the body. Make sure that you are breathing enough, for our relationship with God, like all relationships, takes time.

What is prayer?

Theologian and author Martin Laird writes in his book, A *Sunlit Absence*, that the "reason for our ignorance of the most obvious and simplest of facts about our spiritual life is the constant inner noise and chatter that creates and sustains the illusion of being separate from God, who, as Saint Augustine reminds us, is already, 'closer to me than I am to myself.'"

I have a relatively new vacuum cleaner. It is light and easy to carry, which makes me want to clean more (well, not that much more). But even after just a year and a half of use, it has gotten clogged. It doesn't suction the way that it should, so I took it apart this morning. Yuck. I pulled out lots of dirt and dog hair. Now it works better.

Prayer is more of an unclogging than it is anything else. God adores you and is communicating with you all the time, but, as pure love, God is like light. That light shines onto us constantly, like the sun, but we block it with our confusing thoughts and distracted minds. We block the light with years of habits and obsessions and busyness. True prayer is less about the big list of needs or wants that we want to send to God and more of an unclogging so that the communication can flow between us as it was always meant to do.

Prayer happens when we become conscious of the relationship we have with God. We don't really have to invite God into our lives as God is already there. Prayer just acknowledges that eternal presence. Prayer happens when we awaken to what is already there and begin to interact with the divine reality within and around us. Prayer is when we get stuff out of the way enough to realize that God is there waiting for us.

An Indigenous shaman sits cross-legged out in a field as the sun is setting and feels the cool air as the sun sets. She listens to the sounds of the animals and the birds, the smells of the changing of a season. She feels the solid earth beneath her body. This is prayer.

The Jewish rabbi stands at the Wailing Wall. He wears what some consider strange clothes with strings dangling from his sides. Long curls of hair escape from his yarmulke. He sways, closing his eyes and murmuring. He asks for the salvation of the whole world and of his people. He remembers the ancient story of Israel. This is prayer.

An elderly woman sits at a potter's wheel. Silently she molds the clay as the wheel turns. Her fingers shape the mound, a smooth flowing bowl takes shape. She lets her imagination run and closes her eyes. What does the clay feel like in her hands? What is the shape that is emerging? This is prayer.

An elderly gentleman digs with his hands in rich soil. There he plants a bulb that he hopes will emerge from the ground when the spring approaches. He is lost in concentration, picturing the beautiful flowers that will

grow when the snow melts. He feels the chill autumn
air; his hands have felt this soil for many years. This
is prayer.

There are as many kinds of prayer as there are individuals in this world. Many people don't even realize that they are praying. Art can be prayer. Depth of relationship can be prayer. Walking in nature can be prayer. Music can be prayer; dancing, painting, and even vacuuming can become prayer. What makes it prayer? These activities and others become prayer when there's an open channel of communication, an open heart, a way for God to enter and engage with us. Prayer is a state of awareness.

Yet for all the different types of prayer, there is only one way to begin to pray. Begin by realizing that God has always been there, loving you and patiently waiting for you to awaken to her presence. Wake up. God is here. God has always been here. See, introduce yourself.

The best kind of prayer is a conscious encounter. Think about what you do when you spend time with another person. You sit down for a meal, talk to them, take walks with them; you listen to them, look them in the eye, and give them your attention. You read what they have written and listen to their music. You dance to their songs and rest in their love. Prayer is simply turning your full attention to God. It is giving God the gift of your attention.

Find out how your mind would best receive God's presence. When are you most awake? In the morning? At night? When is your mind alert? Do you love to sing or paint or walk or read or write or dance? What makes your heart sing, and how can you bring God with you to join you in the things that you love to do most? Prayer is best begun where you love to be. Make a beautiful space in your home. Find the best coffee, a comfy chair, a window to look out, a piano to play. Whatever makes your heart sing, go there. That is where prayer begins.

Start slowly and gently and give yourself lots of room for mistakes. There are no shoulds allowed. Give your mind the freedom to jump around like a monkey. Don't get discouraged by your own ability to be distracted. The hardest part of prayer is being bound by our own limitations. Simply put, we disappoint ourselves, and we often give up rather than admit that we are frail, distracted creatures. We cannot experience God without first having to face our own inadequacies. The only person that stands between you and God is yourself. Love your broken self. Start there, and you have a chance.

Prayer is enriched profoundly when you give God your time each day, every day. Breathe in. Breathe out. Give God ten minutes, twenty minutes. Devote this time solely to God. Within the framework of a set period, let your heart lead you. Do you want to paint God a picture? Do you want to say something in writing to God? Do you want to stare at a flower or a tree or a picture of someone you are grateful for? Do you want to light a candle? Devote this time to God and see what happens. But you must do this daily, for several months at the very least. Your mind needs time to quiet and make room for God. Give yourself the benefit of the doubt. Give yourself guilt-free time, free of scolding or criticism. Be patient. Breathe.

One of the greatest enemies of prayer is not distraction: it is guilt. Do not shame yourself or make yourself feel inadequate. Any attempt at prayer does in fact please God. Showing up is what's important, and even when you don't show up, God is fine. We pray because we need to pray, not because God needs us to pray. God is just fine. We are the ones who need it. And if you don't think that you need to pray, then it is not your time yet. Do not pray unless you yearn for God or for the well-being of another person. Guilt can pour acid on your prayer life, so leave it at the door. I would rather have you not pray at all than shame yourself into prayer. God loves you. And you long for God. Let that longing lead you into freely choosing God.

Preparing your mind

To prepare you to enter silence, I want to spend some time focusing on the warfare that goes on in the human mind. I call it warfare because voices of shame and self-criticism wage battles within every human being. We do ourselves a disservice if we simply call these thoughts and impulses things like anxiety, depression, fear. These psychological terms are accurate, but they are ultimately inadequate because they do not do justice to the fact that these thoughts *do not belong to us.* These impulses, feelings, and thoughts come from *outside of us.* They are not part of the person that God created us to be. Often, they come from childhood trauma, destructive cultural influences, conflict, and danger. They are much less present in a well-loved and protected child. But this world is so broken that one cannot live in it without experiencing pain and fear. With this understanding, I call these destructive thoughts and feelings "demons." It is a demon who tells the alcoholic to drink. Yes, alcoholism is an addiction, a disease. But I also see it as a demon. What other word is adequate for a repetitive impulse that tries to kill a human being with alcohol?

I consider suicidal thoughts as demons. The person who hears them must battle these destructive thoughts. It is imperative that the person who hears these destructive thoughts and impulses understands that they do not belong to them, and they are not to blame for having these thoughts. These demon suicide thoughts should be identified as an enemy, and any feelings of shame associated with having them should be let go.

It is important to seek professional help with these challenges as well as to claim the power and authority that we each have to tell the demon(s) to get lost in the name of Jesus. We all have demons, and we all must learn to cast them away. That is the job of everyone who loves God: to cast aside the darkness and put on the armor of light.

For Practice

Begin by reflecting on these questions. You may want to write down your answers in a journal or private place.

1. Do you have thoughts that tell you that you are ugly, stupid, a failure?

2. Do you berate yourself?

3. Do you have thoughts that repeat themselves?

4. Write down these thoughts verbatim. Come to know their voices. Name them for what they are and then cast them aside. That is the gift of prayer, to clean the mind like we would clean a dirty room and to make it ready to receive the Holy One.

Ways to pray

Prayer is the breath of the spiritual life. Without spending time with the divine, there can be no real relationship. Our first step is to start by finding ways to simply be in the presence of God. Begin by pondering these questions: Do you spend time with God in any way at all? What time do you spend? What time could you devote to God? Start simply.

For Practice

As you read the following sections, consider which kinds of prayer appeal to you. What gives you life? What makes you want to take a deep breath and dive in? What kind of prayer feels life-giving to you?

Centering prayer

One of the most profound kinds of prayer is found in silence, in the simple act of listening to God. The art and practice of centering prayer, or silent prayer, is rigorous and takes great discipline, for the North American mind is trained to be overly active and incessantly talkative. The only way to explore the gift of silence is to allow repetitive worries, distractions, and chats inside our minds simply wash over us. We must wait for them to wear themselves out; we must allow them to swirl around us and then wade through them. We cannot forcefully shut down the mind in a way that won't numb us to God's presence, so we must tolerate the mind's jumping and dancing until eventually, it tires or pauses or rests for a moment.

When the prophet Elijah came to the mountain, he was looking for God. He sat in a cave and waited. Great events of nature came to him in wind and fire, and he did not find God in them. Elijah found God *in the still small voice*, or so it was translated from the Hebrew into the King James English. But the translation, like so many translations, butchered the rich and vast meaning of the original Hebrew. When I was in seminary, my Old Testament professor had a new translation for these Hebrew words. He chose the phrase: *eloquent silence*. Once I heard these words, they rang out like a bell in my soul. Of course, Elijah found the presence of God in eloquent silence! That sounds right.

A lot of prayer has to do with trusting ourselves. You are the only one who can experience the movement within your own mind. Only you can know the sound of the voice of love within your mind and distinguish it from the sound of worry or criticism or just factual knowledge. Only you can find the myriad of ways that your mind seeks rest, the traumas it processes, the wisdom it has absorbed. Only you know the different aspects of your mind: the creative side, the worrying mind, the stressed mind. One reason many of us avoid prayer is that we cannot pray without running straight into our own minds and selves. To begin to pray is first to discover our own complexity and inadequacy and then to move beyond that in love. That is why the church talks so much about sin—not because humans are bad in any way. We are good. God said so at the beginning of creation. But sin means that we miss the mark. We are distracted, misled, confused. Once we acknowledge that we are distracted creatures of God, we receive the grace to love ourselves. Sin is just a way of naming our brokenness and learning to accept it.

You cannot pray if you don't want to know yourself. God loves you and calls you inward so that you can then move outward into the world. That is why Jesus, immediately after his baptism, goes out into the desert to pray. And when he is in the desert, scripture is clear that Jesus is tempted by Satan. He hears evil. He is tempted to make food for himself, to worship power, to defy God. Even Jesus is tempted! So why should we be ashamed of our crazy, destructive, lustful, bizarre thoughts? Thoughts don't belong to us, and they don't define us. Even when Eve was free of sin, she was tempted. Temptation happens. It is part of the created order, present even in Eden.

It is important to recognize that Jesus doesn't begin his public ministry until he knows the inner workings of his own mind and faces the temptations of the devil. Only once he comes to an awareness of the nature of his distraction does he emerge to do the work of God. Only after he dismisses the devil can he become the fullness of who God calls him to be. So, we too must navigate and ultimately learn to maneuver past our temptations so that we can fully engage with God. Prayer must come before and during all things. And we cannot pray without confronting our own complex and broken and beautiful minds.

Centering prayer adopts the practice of silence head on. By sitting still, we come face to face with our distractions, temptations, and eventually, as the mind begins to rest, we encounter the presence of the Eternal One. The first step in centering prayer is to find a word. This word must come from the depths of your heart. It should evoke trust, vulnerability, and holiness. It is your own personal word, uttered in the privacy of your mind. It can be used to call the mind back to the center when the mind inevitably wanders. Once you choose a word or phrase, don't second-guess it. The choice of the word is not important; what is important is that you stick with it and try to move more deeply into love with each utterance. One of the first ways the mind may choose to distract is to question the validity of the word itself. Such is worry. It will latch on to whatever is placed before it.

Centering prayer is simply creating silence and protected time for the presence of the holy to become felt and known. But it is one of the most demanding kinds of prayer because it lays us bare in a time when the human mind is used to stimulation. The mind will rebel at first. It will kick and scream and think of every reason why we need to cut the prayer time short and do something else. This

Vital Signs of Faith: GOD

temptation will never leave you, so you must come up with an ironclad method of accountability. You cannot battle this kind of temptation without the motivation of others who will support you as well as hold you accountable. Gather a small group of prayer practitioners to talk with weekly. Tell them how your practice is going. If a group doesn't work, then make yourself accountable to at least other human beings. You cannot do this by yourself. Just ask anyone who battles alcoholism or addiction, for they know what it is to battle temptation. You need your group and your sponsor. We can't do this battle alone. Our minds are addicted to distraction. There is no way to do this alone.

The darkness will not rest until you start praying so find a way to approach this practice with seriousness, rigor, and commitment. This is no joke. It is a battle for your heart and mind. And just as the devil tempted Jesus, so you will be tempted. Every kind of excuse and self-hatred will enter your mind, not just at first but every time you sit down. The devil would much rather have you busy, distracted, and spinning in circles than see you talk with God, listen to your thoughts, and reflect on your life. Centering prayer may look passive, but it is one of the most active things that you can do with your life. To pray in silence is to acknowledge the battle for your attention and time. Centering prayer looks that battle in the face and helps you take the first step to loving yourself anyway.

For Practice

Begin to practice centering prayer by choosing a time of day. Are you a morning person or an evening person? When is your mind at its most clear? When can you carve out protected quiet time? Is there a space in your home or office where you can be still? All electronics must be silenced, or there is no hope for the silencing of the mind.

Begin with five minutes and gradually build up to more. Even 10 minutes a day of sheer silence will alter your life. Be patient and begin slowly but make this time sacrosanct. It must be protected from all forms of distraction. Silence, like breath, is something that we desperately need. You will recognize your hunger for silence once you taste its richness in prayer.

Walking prayer

For many people, praying in silence is too much at first. The mind is simply too noisy. But there are other kinds of prayer, many others. One of them is simply walking.

To walk in nature can be a powerful kind of prayer. When we move the body, it becomes easier to quiet the mind. The simple act of moving the body and looking at the beauty of our natural surroundings can draw the heart and mind to God. The earth is God's canvas, God's masterpiece. It is chock-full of expressions of God's love, from the sounds of geese to the sight of a bright red leaf falling from a tree in autumn. Trees, wind, rocks, grass—all can serve as windows into God's glory. All we need do is walk outside to see this other world, where all of life is interconnected.

If you want to walk and pray, the recipe is simple. Turn off your phone, listen to the sounds of nature, look around at the events of the natural world, and breathe with an even rhythm. You may want to repeat a sacred word that opens the heart or simply listen to the birds, the whisper of snow falling, the wind in the trees, or the rustle of grass. You may focus on your breath, breathing in and out, remembering the pouring out of God's love into you. Most importantly, take the first step (literally!). Then keep walking, remaining open to the experiences around you.

Walking is best done daily. The wonderful part of walking is that it can be both exercise and prayer. The two need not be separated: the body can be active while the mind quiets. In fact, this recipe of moving the body while quieting the mind is a good way for beginners to pray. Walking gives the mind a function, and so the remainder of the mind can quiet more easily.

To walk outside is to pray alongside nature. Each day is unique and new, each sunrise, each moment. With practice, walking becomes a kind of silent love affair with all that God has made, a dance of sorts. Remember that the name *Yahweh*, the ancient Hebrew name for God, sounds very much like the inhalation and exhalation of the breath. When we breathe, we take in God. In the ancient Hebrew, the word for spirit, *ruach*, is the same as the word for breath. To breathe is to literally take in God.

Walking can also have purpose and direction. It can lead to travel and the ancient practice of pilgrimage. You may take your prayers to the Santiago de Compostela in Spain, the Appalachian trail, or the Sinai desert. There is no end to the journeys that can be made. Walking to a holy destination is as ancient as Abraham. God sometimes calls us to walk, to journey. Jesus walked everywhere, and the earliest Christians called themselves a People of the Way. To walk is to use your body to move toward God. It is a rich and powerful form of prayer.

When I hiked in the Sinai desert, the silence was deafening, and the simple sound of my own footsteps was all that I could hear. I heard my own thoughts and temptations with a clarity that I had never experienced before.

Walking along the Sea of Galilee, I felt that I could almost see Jesus as he too walked the same worn paths two thousand years ago. To walk in the footsteps of Jesus or of the saints is to literally follow with the body, mind, and heart.

There was a man in my parish whose accomplished wife died tragically of a cancerous brain tumor when she was only in her fifties. Their life-giving marriage was cut short, and he found himself in the depths of grief. Medications and therapy did not seem to help so he decided to walk the Camino, the pilgrimage to Santiago de Compostela in Spain. It took him months. It was exhausting and scary, but his mind and heart began to rest, and the pain began to ease. One day, while walking miles alone, he saw two images of his wife: one was healthy and vibrant as she was before her illness, the other was sickly and fighting for her life. These two persons merged into one, and they walked beside him for a while. When he returned from his pilgrimage, my friend's grief had relaxed a bit. It was still there, his love for her and his missing her, but she had walked alongside him, and he could now walk on into the rest of his life.

For Practice

Do you love to walk or run? Are you physically able to do so? What kind of time could you spend daily walking or running outside? If you can take this time, follow your breath. Listen to the sounds of nature. Be present as your body moves and experience the quieting of your mind. Practice this walking prayer daily to renew both body and mind.

Intercession and gratitude

It is important that we also give ourselves permission to talk to God. If this relationship with our Maker is in fact the breath of the spiritual life, then we must spend time communicating with the Holy One. And we need to learn to talk to God.

It may feel strange at first to pray aloud or even to talk to God silently in your mind. But in your prayers, you can and should ask God for what you want, for what you wish for the world and for your loved ones. To intercede on another's behalf, to pray for someone, is a powerful act of love. When I tell a person that I will pray for them, I take that seriously. It is sometimes the only thing that I can do for them. But to pray for people and for the world, I must also come to some kind of understanding about how God might answer these prayers. For if we pray and do not contemplate how God might answer, we can get frustrated or even believe that the act of prayer is futile.

All who engage in intercessory prayer will, at some point, ask the question: "Does God really hear my prayers?" People have asked me this time and again throughout my ministry as a priest, and when I reassure them that yes, God does in fact hear their prayers, they ask me when and how God answers. The best response to these deep and profound questions lies in the words of Jesus himself. When trying to describe our relationship with God, Jesus speaks in parables. These parables are his attempt to explain the unexplainable, to fathom the unfathomable, to share eternal truths to temporal minds. These parables are simple and yet deep, accessible and yet profound.

One parable, in particular, addresses how God answers prayer better than any other explanation I have ever heard. Here are the words of Jesus as he tells this parable:

> The kingdom of God is as if someone would scatter seed on the ground, and would sleep and rise night and day, and the seed would sprout and grow, he does not know how. The earth produces of itself, first the stalk, then the head, then the full grain in the head. But when the grain is ripe, at once he goes in with his sickle, because the harvest has come. (Mark 4:26-29)

It's helpful to think about the "kingdom of God" through the Greek term, *basileia*, which means the realm of God, the presence of God, the rule of God. Basically, Jesus is trying to tell us what it's like to be in relationship with God, to live in God's domain. Jesus says that when we enter into a relationship with God, seeds are planted. When we pray, we plant a seed in the mind of God and in our lives. Just as we cannot see a seed under the ground, so we often cannot tell if God has heard us at all. But from the minute we utter a prayer, that seed is sown, and it is growing and changing. From the moment we utter a prayer, the prayer is beginning to be answered.

But the God of the Universe, who formed the stars and established the seas, does not act like a fast-food drive-through or a vending machine. God's answers can take years, decades, millennia. God is eternal, and God's answers will be known in their fullness only in God's time.

Jesus acknowledges that once the seed starts to sprout, and we can see something coming out of the ground, the plant may be nothing like the fullness of what we expected. The seed for wheat starts as a small green shoot, then there is a stalk, then a head on the stalk and, only after it is fully developed, does the grain of wheat become what it was intended to be. Once the grain is fully itself, the farmer recognizes it immediately and takes it for the harvest.

So, it is with our prayers. First, we ask, then often we see nothing, then maybe something is observed but it is nothing like what we asked for. Over time, that answer keeps changing and developing until our prayer is answered more fully and completely than we could have imagined.

There is a book written about my great uncle, Hiram Bingham IV. He was the diplomatic attaché to France right before World War II. Uncle Harry, as we knew him, became alarmed by how the Jews were being treated in Germany and by the spread of anti-Semitism. He appealed to the US government to issue visas to Jews so they could leave Europe, but government officials were still trying to negotiate with Adolph Hitler. So, Uncle Harry began to issue visas illegally. He managed to help more than 1,000 Jews emigrate to the United States before the government discovered what he was doing. The government officials fired Harry and sent him home to Connecticut in disgrace.

By the time I knew Uncle Harry, he was old and a bit senile. He and his wife, Rose, had eleven children, and Harry was prone to painting landscapes in his bathroom. Rose drank too much and would visit my family just to talk. She never said as much, but I imagine she had asked God for her husband to be recognized for his courage. Instead, Uncle Harry died of old age in obscurity.

Years after his death, the White House invited Harry's eleven children and their children and even his great grandchildren to a special ceremony, and Uncle Harry was given a medal of honor posthumously. Aunt Rose's prayer was finally heard, and I suspect she smiled down from heaven. The recognition he received was broader and wider after his death, as Harry had so many offspring, many of whom had no idea what he had done. The story of his courage will now be passed down for generations to come.

It has taken me the better part of my 51 years to see God answering some of my prayers, but answers have come. They just seem to come in God's time and not according to my calendar. One of my oldest prayers is for God to take my life and let me serve. God answers that prayer every day in deeper and deeper ways. God never stops answering.

When you pray, don't think for a moment that God doesn't hear you. God hears every word, just like God counts the hairs on your head. But prayer is like planting seeds, and you cannot rush the Holy One, nor can you always understand what God is doing. Once we realize that God's answers take time and are completely out of our control, we can begin to look and watch for those answers with new awareness—and the answers begin to pour in. Just last night, I was praying for my fear to be lessened while walking my dog. Just as the prayer entered my mind, I passed by a small free library. I felt the urge to look inside and discovered a book called *Fearless: How to Move Beyond Our Fears*. That time, the answer came at once. Sometimes, the answer takes longer than my lifetime. But the answer always comes.

Be assured that no prayer is ever lost or goes unanswered. The answer may be unrecognizable at times, but one day, you will see that answer and understand its fullness, even if you are watching from heaven by then. Never stop praying to God for things that may seem impossible to you: for reconciliation among people who can't see past their differences, for an end to war and the pollution of our planet, for things that seem impossible to achieve. Ask and ask and ask again. Plant those seeds and understand that the Maker of all things has a plan much greater than anything that we can understand or fathom.

And if you find yourself searching for the right words, turn to the beautiful Book of Common Prayer or lean on the words of Jesus himself in the Lord's prayer. Just speak to God. God listens.

There is another way to talk to God and that is to articulate the things for which you are thankful. Gratitude can alter the way that we see the world. This kind of prayer will be described in greater detail in the section on giving, but it is an essential component to the life of prayer. Say aloud or think of the simple words "thank you" each time life blesses you in some way. The act of saying thanks calls attention to the positive aspects of life and can train our brains to see the good. It can change our perception of our lives. Teach a young child to give thanks at the end of each day, and it will shape the way that this child sees the world.

For Practice

For intercession prayers, begin by making a short list of people who may need some help—the sick, the lonely, the grieving. Say their names aloud. If you have a wish for them, say that too. Speak aloud at first, and then move the prayers into your mind. Make this kind of prayer a part of your daily practice. It will connect you in love to those for whom you pray. And then watch for God to answer.

For prayers of gratitude, simply name before God the things for which you are grateful at the end of each day.

Worship and corporate prayer

Worship is an act of defiance, for it is one of the most impractical things a person can do. Amid our busy lives, in which we are pressured to accomplish tasks, worship happens when we set aside time and space from the regular world. We step outside of the world of doing and allow ourselves to simply be in the presence of God together as a community.

For many, worship means dressing up in our finest, singing songs, and encountering God. But I like to define worship as a conversation. It is a form of prayer—but not between a person and God but between two or more people and God. And I believe that worship, more than anything else on this earth, is what human beings were created to do.

Evelyn Underhill, an early twentieth-century Christian mystic, describes this sentiment well in her book, *Worship*, though her terms are now outdated.

> Man, incited by God, dimly or sharply conscious of the obscure pressure of God, responds to him best not by a simple movement of the mind; but by a rich and complex action, in which his whole nature is concerned, and which has at its full development the characters of a work of art.

Worship unites human beings to one another, not by forcing us to analyze or even speak to each other but by uniting us in a common activity: to gaze upon, sing to, listen to, and be fed by God. The psalmist of ancient Israel once sang these words of instruction to us: "Worship the Lord in the beauty of holiness" (Psalm 96:9).

In worship, we see beauty, hear beauty, smell beauty, and taste beauty. And while all of this is happening, we also sense that there is so much more going on that is beyond our sight. From time to time, we feel deep inside an immense presence among us. And Jesus's words from the Gospel of Matthew become incarnate, enfleshed and made manifest among us: "For where two or three are gathered in my name, I am there among them" (Matthew 18:20).

The importance of gathering is reflected even in some of the rules of our tradition. For instance, as a priest, I am unable to consecrate the bread and wine in my tradition if I am alone. I must have another human soul present. The potency of God's presence is simply not the same without another person. Indeed, there is a strength in the worshipping community. This plays out even within the family structure. Families that worship together create a bond, a rootedness that supports a vital spiritual life. I believe there is no more valuable way to spend your time than sitting with your family or your loved ones in a house of worship.

Why does worship matter? When we come together to offer praise and thanks to God, we fulfill a primal need within all human beings to stand in the presence of the holy and to acknowledge the mystery of life itself and our boundedness within it. We are made to acknowledge the numinous nature of the life that we have been given and we are meant to do that in community.

There are many types and styles of worship across religious traditions and within religious traditions. In each of the major world religions, there are those who are highly ritualistic and those who prefer simplicity or discussion. There are liturgies geared toward an emotional experience and those that are more about simply practicing the routine laid before you. The reason for so many expressions of worship is not our failure to get along so much as our need to express that which is deep within us. We do not expect art forms to be the same; why would we demand that worship be the same? Indeed, art, music, dance, and theater all have a similar purpose as worship. The Eastern Orthodox call the liturgy "The Divine Drama," an understanding that good liturgy, good worship, is art directed to its true source.

There is no right or wrong when it comes to liturgy so long as it is a genuine attempt to pray. I do not believe for a second that the master of the universe cares if we stand or sit or kneel, if we raise our hands and sing rock and roll or kneel in penitence and chant. What matters is that the method of worship resounds in our hearts and opens our hearts to the presence of God.

Worship is the acknowledgment of the presence of the Almighty among the people. It is the establishment of right relationship between the human and the Creator. No wonder I often feel as if I have been somehow aligned again after I worship. It reminds me of doing yoga when my back has been strained. Yoga will often realign my spine. Sometimes I can even crack my spine as it gets into alignment. And then I want to laugh, and I feel so much better. That is the way that I feel about worship. It realigns my life. And when I don't go, things in my life feel mysteriously out of sync. My priorities get skewed. I feel off balance. When I don't worship regularly, I slowly make myself too important. I become the center of my universe, and I start getting lost and afraid. Worship is my source of clarity, realignment, and strength.

For Practice

Where can you find a place to worship? If you do not have a church home, visit some. Think of it as a blind date. Where do you fall in love? What kind of worship makes your heart sing and moves you? Remember, you are not seeking perfection, only a true connection wherein you feel God's presence in community.

If you already have a church community, commit to regular attendance at worship services. As you make worship a priority in your life, reflect upon how worship helps realign your heart and spiritual life.

Where people pray together

The culture and educational system of the contemporary West are based almost exclusively upon the training of the reasoning brain and, to a lesser degree, of the aesthetic emotions. Most of us have forgotten that we are not only brain and will, senses and feelings; we are also spirit. Modern man has for the most part lost touch with the truest and highest aspect of himself; and the result of this

inward alienation can be seen all too plainly in his
restlessness, his lack of identity and his loss of hope.
—Kallistos Ware, *The Orthodox Way*

God blesses everything he creates, and, in biblical
language, this means that he makes all creation the
sign and means of his presence and wisdom, love and
revelation: "O Taste and See that the Lord is good."
—Alexander Schmemann, *For the Life of the World*

From the beginning of recorded history, human beings
have set aside places in which to encounter God. If you
traveled the globe and looked at these spaces, no matter the
religious tradition, you would see that they were beautiful,
special, different, transcendent, wholly other.

Think of the great mosques of the Middle East. Picture
Hindu temples, Buddhist shrines, Christian churches—no
matter what the religion, we want to set aside a beautiful
place for God. As Mircea Eliade, anthropologist and religious
historian, writes in her book, *The Sacred and the Profane*,
"Man becomes aware of the Sacred because it manifests
itself, shows itself, as something wholly different from the
Profane." Further, we don't so much create these spaces as
we find them. We find a sacred space, a piece of ground that
feels set apart, and we build a piece of art or architecture
upon it to express its majesty.

The temple of Israel was a work of art and of awe, and Jews
believed that it reflected the majesty of the entire cosmos.

It was, quite literally, a focal point, a meeting place for the divine to touch earth, the eternal to meet the temporal.

If we were to invite God to dinner, we would certainly clean the house and get out our best china. In the same way, we create these spaces, our most beautiful, transcendent spaces, in which to welcome God. "Here," we say to God, "you live here." How ridiculous and yet how endearing for us to think we could construct "God's house." But we do. We always have.

The cathedral I serve sits upon the highest point in Jacksonville, Florida. Now that there are high rises, this little hill is difficult to identify, but early on, people regarded this area as a sacred space, a place where heaven was closer to earth, a "thin place" as the Celts would call it. The first church building on the hill was dedicated in 1851 but was burned to the ground a few years later in the Civil War. Dedicated to this spot, parishioners rebuilt the building in brick only to have it burn down again in the great fire that swept through Jacksonville in 1901. The third edifice sits on Billy Goat Hill today. That's how important this place was and still is. Christians built not one, not two, but three churches upon it, each one more magnificent than the last, all with an altar at the center, where we could share the bread and wine as Jesus had done at the Last Supper.

From the earliest days, Abraham built an altar to recognize and mark the presence of God. Two thousand years later, we are still building and rebuilding places to gather as faithful people in community. When we experience God, we want to mark the space in which the interaction occurs, the place on this earth where the sacred touched us. We set aside spaces for worship to mark the relationship that is unfolding between humanity and the Creator.

I spent one summer in college researching the Eastern Orthodox liturgy of Saint John Chrysostom in Russia. It was 1990, and the Soviet Union was crumbling. People were punished for going to church; they could be taxed, their children could be taken out of school, and even sent to prison.

Despite the heavy consequences, people still snuck into church. The church I attended was hidden by trees. The entrance was in the back. But people came. And they came with a kind of desperation that I had not seen before.

Upon entering the church, I was struck with the strong smell of incense. Women lit wax candles while a thurifer censed the icons. There was so much movement: kneeling, crossing yourself, standing again. There were no chairs, just some benches on the sides of the worship space for the elderly or those with disabilities.

I realized at the time that we were being exposed to the story of Jesus through all the senses: everywhere you looked you could see icons, beautiful architecture, candles. Music and chanting fed me with holy sounds. Incense stirred our sense of smell, and the eucharist and wine tasted distinctive and memorable. When the wafer touched my mouth, I felt God was placed there to touch my whole being.

All the senses were engaged. And so it is with ancient worship. We are being told a story, told of a relationship with one who wants to reach us, who will try to reach us on every level, through touch and taste and sight and sound, even through smell. God says, "Touch me, taste me, hear me, see me, smell me. I am here."

Just today, I baptized a baby girl. Her cousins came to visit the church, ages two and four. The two boys were absolutely engaged by the holy space of the cathedral. The two-year-old began to yell, loving to hear his voice resonate throughout the large space. The boys ran and danced up and down the aisles, gazed at a dragon in the stained-glass window, put their hands on the marble floor around the altar, and climbed the stone steps to the pulpit. As I watched them play, I realized that this entire beautiful structure that was built so long ago is like one beautiful playground to them. It is a vast space to be enjoyed and explored. I loved to hear their shrieks of laughter and the sounds of their joy as they explored. "This is God's house," I said to them. "It is very big, and God loves it when you play here."

Those little boys were young enough to allow the space to speak to them. They were joyful and awe inspired. Could we not be the same?

For Practice

Find a beautiful worship space somewhere that you can attend regularly. Sit alone in this space and see how it speaks to you. Attend services there. You will be fed spiritually by this holy space simply by standing within it with an open heart.

Eating and fasting

Centuries of secularism have failed to transform eating into something strictly utilitarian. Food is still treated with reverence... To eat is still something more than to maintain bodily functions. People may not understand what that 'something more' is, but they nonetheless desire to celebrate it. They are still hungry and thirsty for sacramental life.

—Alexander Schmemann, *For the Life of the World*

Our culture is ill about many things, but chief among them is the way we view our bodies and our relationship to food. Food is meant to be earned and cultivated, to be savored and appreciated. It is a vital part of our physical health. But many of us struggle with our relationship with food. Some have too little food, while others have too much. Some seek false comfort in food or battle food-related diseases like obesity and anorexia. Our relationship with food is complicated by our economic structures. The rich have the resources and access to healthy food choices, able to afford organic produce and delicacies that come in small portions. Meanwhile the poor often live in food deserts, shopping for groceries at gas stations or convenient markets and making do with fatty, processed foods. Consequently, the poor are disproportionately overweight and unhealthy, creating a further gap in health and well-being.

Food is presented to us as if it is free and has no value. Buffets overwhelm eaters. Fast food promotes the illusion that it takes no time to prepare food. Even food pantries, with the noble goal of giving food away to battle hunger, contribute to this disconnect. We are all confused when it comes to eating and our bodies. Instead of seeing food as a gift that sustains life, we see it as something to take for granted, something that is abundant and almost meaningless. We lose the sense of gratitude and the miracle that occurs when we nourish our bodies with food. We forget that every piece of lettuce, every bean or piece of chicken has come from a miraculous process of growth and development that could not happen without God's grace and the beauty of this created world. Food connects us to the earth and to one another. The more we divorce ourselves from what food really is and where it came from, the more we lose a sense of who we are in relationship to God our Creator.

From Adam and Eve, who ate what was not freely offered to them, to Jesus, who offered us his very body and blood to eat, there is no denying that eating and food are an intrinsic part of the life of faith. Jesus says that what we eat does not determine our character: It is not what goes into the mouth that defiles a person, but it is what comes out of the mouth that defiles (Matthew 15:11). Nevertheless, what we eat impacts our bodies and our moods. We cannot come to know God when our bodies are at war with our minds, and food can be the fuel that ignites the war.

Ironically, one way to address our relationship with food is through fasting, that is, abstaining from food for a period of prayer and intense focus on God. We see this type of prayer modeled by Jesus. He fasted regularly. It was the first thing he did after his baptism. The gospels of Matthew, Mark, and Luke all record how Jesus withdrew to the desert after his baptism for forty days fasting and prayer. As Christians, we recall Jesus's sacrifice during the forty days of the season of Lent. Often, we might give up chocolate or something for Lent to remember what Jesus did in the desert. But Jesus didn't just give up chocolate (they didn't even have it back then!). Jesus stopped eating entirely. This was his way of radically praying. To fast is to spend a focused kind of attention on God, without the distraction of food. It is an advanced form of prayer which can serve to deepen our relationship with God.

Let me offer a word of caution here: you cannot fast until your relationship with food has become a healthy relationship. Fasting is the last step. If you are still working through your relationship with food, begin by learning to prepare a meal. Cook something from scratch. Wait for it, appreciate it. Give thanks during grace at that meal—and every meal. These are places to start repairing and building a healthy relationship with food. Just as with any of the vital signs of the spiritual life, your relationship with food is unique and individual to you. Begin where you are. If you overeat or have an eating disorder, if you have health issues of any kind, be careful and consult both doctors and mental health professionals first. The goal of fasting is to be both healthy physically and to gain a new awareness of God. It is never about losing or gaining weight. It has nothing to do with what your body looks like. Fasting is about your health, both physically and spiritually. So, take care of yourself and if there is any shame or guilt involved, back off. Just like with other forms of prayer, shame is the enemy of the spiritual life. Fasting because you are ashamed of your body is not fasting. There is a big difference between dieting and fasting. You must only fast from a place of love, for yourself and your body and for God.

Once you feel ready to pray by fasting, it's helpful to think of the practice as a time of refraining. We refrain from something so that we can recognize its role in our lives and become conscious of our use of it. Most Americans eat rather unconsciously. When the pandemic hit, one of the ways I comforted myself was to watch movies and eat a bag of chips or a bowl of ice cream. It felt like I was treating myself, and the food tasted great, but it left me feeling bad, bloated, and even lonelier. I ate way more than I intended, making trips back and forth from my sofa to the kitchen without even thinking about it. It seemed like the food was calling to me, and I wasn't even hungry.

When a person dies, in many of the world's religions, people gather after a service of worship to eat together. We do this because food is still a sign of life for us. The dead do not eat. By eating, we are affirming life. It is a way of recognizing that we are living, breathing creatures of God who need nourishment. Food is the fuel that keeps us alive. Only water is more important to us. When someone is dying, they stop eating. It is a natural way for the body to shut down. To eat, then, is to embrace life.

So, why do we fast? We fast so that we can eat with reverence and appreciation. We also fast because once the pangs of hunger subside, we discover a peace of mind that comes when the digestive tract truly rests. Studies have shown that fasting can even be a healthy way for the body to quiet and pause.

Jesus knew when to fast, and he knew when to eat. On the night before he died, of all the things that he could have done (remember that he alone knew he was going to die the next day), Jesus chose to eat a meal with his friends. By feeding his friends, Jesus demonstrated his love for them in a way that has resounded through the centuries.

When a baby is frightened, we usually hold the baby and put something in their mouth. The need to be fed is so deeply primal, so preverbal that we could not begin to unpack its ramifications for each one of us. To feed someone is to love them. It is to say to them, "I want you to live." "I want you to survive." Bread is life. Food is life. Jesus fed us before he died, and he fed us with himself, his own body and blood. He said, "I in them, and you in me" (Jesus 17:23). Like a fetus feeds off their mother, Jesus tells us that it is God who nourishes us, not just spiritually but also physically. God loves us and wants us to live, even beyond death.

We fast so that we may eat with the conscious understanding that food is not to be taken for granted, that it is a profound spiritual act to eat. We fast so that we may eat with an awareness of the gift of life itself.

For Practice

Begin by asking yourself these questions. What is your relationship to food? Do you understand that eating and fasting can both be forms of prayer? If this concept is new to you, begin by saying grace and giving thanks each time that you eat. Try simply gazing at a beautiful plate of food before you eat. Give thanks for its beauty. Then, once you begin to eat, savor the taste of the food. If there are others eating with you, look at them, listen to their stories. The community that forms around a table is eucharistic and infused with God's love. It can become a place of transformation.

Finding your way to pray

I hope this section on God has convinced you that prayer is like your breath: it is one of the essential aspects of the spiritual life. Without prayer, there can be no life with God. But there are as many ways to pray as snowflakes in the sky or sand in the sea. Your way will be uniquely yours, and it will change as you grow and develop.

The best way to start is simply to start. Do not scold yourself for any attempt. If your mind wanders, try walking or running. God is pleased with any attempt that we make to spend time alone with our Lord! Be good to yourself. Just try.

ALMIGHTY GOD, *we want to come to you. We want to know you and to love you, but we do not know how to begin. Guide us to find ways to nurture our relationship with you. Help us to create space in our homes for prayer, and times of quiet. Give us the strength to put down our cell phones and to-do lists, even if just for a few minutes, so that we can simply breathe and allow you to enter our hearts with each breath. Thank you for creating in us a desire to find you. Awaken that desire in us and nurture it so that we may breathe in your Holy Spirit more and more. Amen.*

GIVE
The Pulse

> Your heart rate, or pulse, can guide you to discover dangerous health conditions that need expert care, such as some heart problems. But your normal resting heart rate changes throughout your life as you age.
>
> —OnHealth.com, "Heart Health: What is a Healthy and Normal Heart Rate for My Age?"

The heart is a magnificent organ, located at the very center of the human body, pumping blood throughout the organs. The rate at which the heart pumps is one of the major indicators of the health of the body. When the body exerts itself, through exercise or fighting illness, the heart rate increases. A strong heart makes a larger impact on the body with one single beat, whereas the weak heart must beat more frequently to do its job.

The pulse is easy to measure and detect. It is there for all to hear. Any person can take their pulse at any time. There is no hiding from the honesty of the heart.

In biblical times, the heart was seen as the source of intelligence and feeling. To have a pure heart was to draw closer to God. The psalmist prayed, Create in me a clean heart, O God, and renew a right spirit within me (Psalm 51:11).

And in the beginning of the eucharistic worship, the priest begins with this prayer,

> Almighty God, to you all hearts are open, all desires known, and from you no secrets are hid: Cleanse the thoughts of our hearts by the inspiration of your Holy Spirit, that we may perfectly love you and worthily magnify your holy Name, through Christ our Lord. Amen. (The Book of Common Prayer, p. 355)

Just as the heart pumps life and blood to the organs, so the act of giving makes our convictions become reality. Giving moves the faithful person from thought and intention to action: it is an activity that can express the health of the spiritual life while also impacting the world. And giving is so easy to measure. As much as we may try to keep the exact amount of our giving a secret from others, we always know if we gave of our resources and of ourselves. It is clear as day. Just like the pulse, you can measure your giving any time. It is something that we cannot and should not hide from ourselves. This is the second measurable vital sign of the health of the spiritual life.

Divine origins

Give to others and God will give to you.

—Luke 6:38

God is a giver. The act of creation itself is a gift. God gives humanity dominion over all the earth in the book of Genesis. And God gives us Jesus, the Son, whose life and death are a gift that transforms us every day. Part of the essence of divinity, of the life of the Trinity, is the act of giving. When we give to one another and to God, we reflect the divine nature. It is one of the many reasons for which we have been created.

In the second chapter of Genesis, the fall occurs when Eve and Adam take instead of giving. All had been freely given to them but instead of gratitude and generosity, they chose to take what was not given. At the root of our fallen nature is the tendency to take instead of give, to see the world for what we cannot have rather than for what we have, to focus on the glass as being half empty rather than half full.

At the root of much of the brokenness and evil of this world is the perception of emptiness. When people are afraid their needs will not be met, they become paralyzed and stuck. On the one hand, fear can be a healthy motivator. It can prompt us to go out and procure shelter and food for ourselves and others. But when that fear drives us to seek and consume more than we need, then fear twists into greed. And it is greed born of fear that lies at the root of most evils of this world.

The ancient story of the Garden of Eden tells a deep truth about who we are. In the story, Adam and Eve are misled by the serpent. The serpent introduces into their mind the perception of emptiness, of pointing out to them the one thing that they cannot have, and then suggesting they take and consume this forbidden fruit. From the perception of emptiness, the serpent develops a sense of ownership. Take and eat, the serpent instructs. It can be yours.

Before the fall, Adam and Eve own nothing. They receive the gifts of the garden freely and with joy. And no doubt they give God the gifts of joy, innocence, and wonder.
There is a free flow of love between God and humanity. After the fall, Adam and Eve perceive themselves as naked, as needing and wanting possessions. They want to take what isn't given and consume it. The flow of free love in the act of giving and receiving is replaced by the act of wanting and taking. And the rupture in our relationship with God begins.

The idea that we human beings can own anything permanently is distorted. We are creatures who live and breathe for only a short time. We do not own things beyond our lifetimes, and even in our lives, we cannot hold much of what we claim to own. Can you wrap your arms around land? Can you control another human being? Can you even own a piece of fruit? Over time, won't that fruit change and rot within your very grasp? Can you really "hold" it?

The concept of ownership has broken our world. As human beings have tried to amass wealth, we have distorted our relationship with each other and with the planet. We have tried to possess people, animals, land, and even our own children. I think back to the European settlers, landing in Virginia, and taking land that Indigenous peoples were living on. These settlers claimed that they owned the land simply by standing on it, building houses upon it, and murdering its prior inhabitants. But owning land is like trying to wrap our arms around a whale. It is too big for us to hold onto. We don't own the land, and we can't control the weather. We cannot own something so huge and complex and beyond our understanding. It would be like claiming to own a star.

On June 19, 1865, the last of the enslaved people were liberated in Galveston, Texas when 2,000 Union soldiers marched into town. Juneteenth is a day both to honor this day of liberation and repent of the abomination of slavery and the fact that it took us hundreds of years to begin to awaken to its destruction and consequences for all of humanity. Part of the root of this great sin was greed and a distorted understanding of ownership. God forgive us for thinking that we could own another human being. How could we have even conceived of such a thing?

Human nature is never satisfied. Once people have their needs provided, they want more. They begin to convince themselves that they need more. Wants become confused with needs, and what may have begun as simply providing for individual needs begins to oppress others. What we too often fail to see is that ownership at the expense of any person or creature is a recipe for disaster, for we are all interconnected.

Human beings are merely caretakers on this earth, here for a short time. As the psalmist says, we are a breath that comes and goes away. We are not here long, and we cannot possess or hold onto something when we ourselves won't last long enough to grasp it. How can a temporary being hold onto anything? Our bodies are here for a short time. We cannot take anything with us.

Years ago, I heard a story of a man whose wealthy father was dying. His father had been a very successful businessman, rising from poverty to great riches by buying and selling used cars and real estate. The father was proud to raise his son but diligent about never giving the son much money, hoping that the hardship he had endured would also shape the character of his son. Although his father was a millionaire, the son had to work hard to make ends meet. The son did well for himself, never becoming as wealthy as his father but earning a living and providing for his family.

At the age of 65, the father was diagnosed with pancreatic cancer. After battling the disease, he was greatly weakened and eventually had to be put on hospice care. It was time to write his will, something that he had avoided all his life. The stark reality of his death was staring him in the face.

As his father lay dying, the son sat by his bedside in the hospice unit. He noticed his dad's Rolex watch. His dad loved that watch and had worn it as a sign of his success for most of his adult life. For the son, it was a symbol of strength and success and reminded him of his father.

"Dad," the adult son said. "Would you be willing to give me your watch?"

"No, my son," the father said. "I just don't want to give it up."

And so, the father was buried with his Rolex watch, and I suppose the watch now sits by itself in a concrete box, in a mahogany casket, in the ground of a cemetery, the bones of the father having disintegrated.

The man lived under the illusion that he owned the money that he earned, that it was his to hold and to keep. This illusion turned idolatrous. He began to worship his wealth and to confuse it with his identity and purpose. He did not know how to give. He never practiced the art of giving, and it was as if his pulse gradually faded away. The heart of his soul withered without this essential vital sign of the spiritual life. He died without ever experiencing the joy of giving— and without loving his son well. His heart suffered because he did not know how to give. He did not know how to love. As Jesus says so clearly, "You cannot serve God and wealth" (Matthew 6:24b).

The concept of ownership is, at its very essence, flawed. We cannot own as we do not have permanence. We can eat and consume food. We can wear clothes, and we can utilize objects to perform tasks. We can grow plants and care for animals. We can hand over objects and money into the care of others, but we cannot really own, not in a permanent sense. We cannot possess for we do not live long enough to do more than borrow. When we give, we return what is essentially God's in the first place. Just as the pulse pumps living oxygen throughout the body, so giving pumps true life into the soul. We are righted in our relationship with God, the flow of life is made whole once more.

For Practice

Gaze at some of your possessions. Consider how they are not yours but only borrowed for a time.

Jesus's words

In the only prayer that Jesus taught us, he asks God to give us *this day our daily bread*. He does not ask for money but for food. And he doesn't ask for more than what is needed on *this day*. In Jesus's words, we see the model for how we are to live in the present moment. There is no hoarding, no saving, no holding. Just feed us today so that we may live.

In the gospels, Jesus talks more about giving than he does about prayer. When people ask him what they should do, his first response is not to tell them to pray but to tell them to give: if you have two coats, give one away—and do the same with food. I cannot stress this point enough: there is no spiritual health, no true freedom in God without radical giving. When we give, we push back on the greatest of human sin: we fight the lie of ownership, and we begin to right the world. Giving is the very heartbeat of the Christian life.

Jesus tells us that our practice of giving liberates God to give more to us. This is the mystery and the irony of generosity. The more we give, the more God will give to us. Jesus says,

> Give to others, and God will give to you. Indeed you will receive a full measure, a generous helping, poured into your hands- all that you can hold. The measure you use for others is the one that God will use for you.
> —Luke 6:38, Good News Translation

Another way of understanding Jesus's words is to trust that we humans need to give. When we live in fear amid a perception of emptiness or scarcity, we starve ourselves of the true riches of God. We need to give so that God can give to us. If we try to feed ourselves, to provide for ourselves beyond our basic needs, we fill a hole that only God can fill. We replace the divine nourishment of God with useless things like fast food and cosmetic products.

If we know we don't own anything, if we absorb the truth that it is only from God that we have the gift of life, of each breath we take and each day we love and learn, then we can serve the one who gives, accepting God's gifts and asking God to help us give to others. The flow of love is freed once more, and we become full of good news. Our heart is healthy and our pulse steady and strong.

For Practice

Notice what God gives you today. At the end of the day, write down the gifts of God for you, from a beautiful sunrise to a smile from a friend to something you were able to buy.

Gratitude

The preface to this journey of giving has nothing to do with material things. Before we give anything at all, we must alter our perception of our lives. We do this by practicing gratitude, by changing the way we view the things and people around us. We practice gratitude when we choose to acknowledge everything that blesses us, even our pain. I specifically use the word "practice" because saying thank you to God is a practice, a discipline, not a feeling. If we wait to feel something, we are at the whim of our emotions. Instead, as we alter our perception, we begin to see gratitude as a discipline and an art, one practiced simply by naming all the things, people, ideas, and events for which we are grateful.

My cousin Richard lives in Washington, D.C. He is married, has a full-time job as a lawyer with a thriving nonprofit, and is the father of a toddler. Each day, amidst the business of life (trying to raise a toddler in a pandemic is no joke!), Richard practices what he calls "The ABC's". He does the ABC's in the grocery store, in the car, on the train, in his office, whenever he can remember. Here is how you can do them too:

Simply walk through the alphabet and give thanks for that thing in your life that begins with each letter: A, B, C...and so on. It reorients the mind to gratitude. The brilliance of the ABC's of gratitude is that it's a game. Gratitude need not be serious or cumbersome! Have fun with it!

Giving naturally emerges from gratitude, from a sense of abundance, a noticing the gifts God has given us, and then the desire to further the blessings. In her majestic book, *Braiding Sweetgrass*, Robin Wall Kimerer writes about her experience as an Indigenous woman growing up in a culture of gratitude. She explains: "Cultures of gratitude must also be cultures of reciprocity. Each person, human or no, is bound to every other in a reciprocal relationship. Just as all beings have a duty to me, I have a duty to them. If an animal gives its life to feed me, I am in turn bound to support its life. If I receive a stream's gift of pure water, then I am responsible for returning a gift in kind. An integral part of a human's education is to know those duties and how to perform them."

Giving thanks is a way of life. The practice of gratitude turns the mind toward the positive, toward the light. I instruct parents as they prepare for the baptism of their child to teach the child to give thanks every evening before bed. Teach them to look over their day with a grateful eye; this perspective will shape the way they see the world.

For Practice

Try giving thanks daily, or whenever you can think of it. Try working the ABC's of gratitude or giving thanks when your head hits the pillow at the end of the day. Work this practice of gratitude into your daily life and reap the benefits of a new perspective.

How to give

It is almost impossible for North Americans to face the idolatrous notion of ownership that consumes us. It hits too close to home. It is the very fabric upon which our society is built. How can we begin to awaken to this concept when everything in our world tells us to earn and save and own? Where do we even begin? It's so overwhelming that most of us just choose to ignore Jesus's teaching to radical generosity. We might give some small amount and call it a day, patting ourselves on the back for gifts that are not sacrificial and don't affect our wealth.

Is there a way to emerge from this distorted concept of ownership? Is there a way out of the morass that we have created? Can humanity overcome competition and consumption as the primary motivators for our actions? How can we come to another understanding of our role as caretakers of this planet? How do we move toward a way of life that shares with all the riches of this earth?

With God's help, we can take the first steps. We can begin by walking in the way of Jesus and learning to give. When we give, we counteract the self-centered distortion of greed. Every single act of giving is countercultural. Every time you give, you do something radical, something that has the potential to change the world. Just begin, without judgment or shame. This may seem overwhelming because Jesus sets such a high standard, but simply taking the first step of giving is huge.

How can you begin to give as Jesus asks? The first step is to look with honest and objective eyes at your material life. How much money do you have tucked away? What is the worth of your possessions? Begin simply by telling the truth and taking an honest assessment of your material goods— and the other gifts you have been given by God. There is no shame in poverty or riches, but we cannot begin to give if we are unwilling to look with an honest eye at what we have.

Giving of stuff

As far as we know, Jesus did not possess more than the clothes on his own back. Saints throughout the centuries have often begun their life of prayer by first giving away all that they owned. Saint Francis even went so far as to strip off all his clothes and stand naked in the town square! Living lives of simplicity with a minimum of belongings seems to free the mind and soul. It unburdens us.

When my marriage ended, I was left with one son at home and a house full of stuff that summoned mixed memories. My first instinct was to rent a big house and take all the stuff with me. How could I throw away my son's third-grade football trophy? What about their paintings from when they were little? Pictures? My grandmother's silver?

After I moved into the house (and moved all my stuff too!), I was in for a surprise: the people who owned the rental house decided to sell it. I was outraged! I had just moved in! They had to adhere to the one-year lease, but then I was out and there was nothing that I could do about it.

I wondered why. Why did God want me to move again? Hadn't I been through enough? I felt depressed and angry. But I was forced to move, so I began to pack my stuff.

And then, something happened. Here I was, reading about the care of the environment while I packed up all this stuff I never used. What was I doing? Why did I need all this? When my oldest son came home from college, I had decorated his room with trophies and other keepsakes from his childhood. He said, "Mom, this is a shrine to my eight-year-old self. I don't want to stay here." I was devastated, but I realized that he was right. I was holding onto the past just as I held onto my stuff. I needed to let go.

So, I began to purge. I rented a house a third of the size, and I only packed what I felt I used and needed. Everything else had to go. Books, clothes, pots and pans, knickknacks, and on and on. Boxes and boxes. Some people thought I was crazy. You are giving away your dining room table? Are you crazy? But I was finally not crazy. I finally felt a little bit sane.

So here I am, just three days in this new house. And despite all my purging, I still have way more stuff than Jesus. I still live quite high on the hog, but something has been lifted off me. I feel more free and able to move into the next chapter of my life. I feel able to be present.

Can you liberate yourself from some of your stuff? Have you begun to feel that your possessions possess you, that they control you?

I think of the story of a diplomat who was serving in China before the revolution. He and his wife and their two children lived in a beautiful old home filled with lovely antiques. Late one morning, soldiers knocked on their front door and told them in no uncertain terms that they were being sent back to America. The soldiers told them that they could only take 400 pounds of belongings.

The family began making a pile of the things that they needed to bring home. They placed their most precious belongings in the pile: Albert's violin, the vase that belonged to a great-grandmother, a painting they had found on their honeymoon. Soon, the pile was much too big, and the family began to bicker about which objects to take. They were still bickering when the soldiers returned to escort them out of the country. And with just three words, the soldiers completely transformed the family's relationship to their precious belongings. One of the soldiers simply said, "Weigh the children."

The father, the diplomat, would later write that with those three words, all those things became nothing but trash. TRASH.

You cannot bring any of this stuff with you. All that you will bring to God is the love that you hold in your heart. Focus on that and let go of the stuff. It will weigh you down and make you forget what is truly important.

For Practice

Walk around your house or apartment. What things do you use? What things do you simply want? How can you simplify your life and get rid of some of your belongings? Again, move slowly and simply. Be gentle with yourself. How do you feel after unburdening some of the things that you own but no longer need?

Curbing consumption

He who is contented is rich.

—Lao Tzu

Nature is pleased with simplicity.

—Isaac Newton

Our consumption is ruining this planet and its creatures. We must buy less, travel less, consume less. Our future as a human race depends on it. Ironically, the things we do to make ourselves feel comfortable are the very same things that are slowly going to kill us. We must wake up to our relationship with stuff and with land itself. It is not ours.

Nothing is ours. We belong to God. All things belong to God. We are caretakers, and that is enough.

So, how do we curb our consumption? How do we take the pulse of our desires for more?

I love to eat while watching TV. But this is a bad habit because I end up mindlessly eating more that I would normally allow myself. It is the same with purchasing or consumption. The first step toward conscious consumption is awareness. Start watching what you buy. Do you purchase items that you do not need? Could you refrain and give that money away? What about eating out? Coffee (my weakness)? Amazon orders? As you awaken to your consumption, you will naturally want to curb its appetite.

A plastic garbage patch in the Pacific Ocean between California and Hawaii covers about 618,000 miles—about three times the size of France. And this is only one of five enormous plastic accumulation zones in the world. One way to begin to examine our consumption is to look at our use of plastics. For the past year or so, I have been challenging my congregation to practice their faith in the grocery store by only purchasing items that do not use plastic containers. It is surprisingly difficult. But the environmental impact of our reliance on plastic is profound and has implications for generations to come. It will take strength, ingenuity, and sacrifice to wean ourselves from such consumption, but we must find a way. Otherwise, we forgo our role as caretakers to all God has given us and squander the riches of creation.

For Practice

Try a plastic fast (for a month or a season). Depending on your comfort level, you can throttle your engagement.

Beginner level: *Commit to not using plastic bags. Bring reusable bags with you to the grocery store, farmer's markets, and other retail centers. Another beginner step is to stop using straws at restaurants (or at home!).*

Intermediate level: *Refrain from purchasing any plastic bottles for drinking, in addition to doing the beginner level plastic fast.*

Advanced Level: *Try not to purchase plastic at the grocery store or anywhere else. This is difficult, but it can be done!*

Another great exercise for embracing giving is to make a habit of picking up an extra bag of groceries every time you shop. Give this extra bag to the local food pantry or to your church for distribution. This simple discipline of one extra bag will alter your awareness of the opulence that lies before you. As you practice purchasing one extra bag, you will be formed, shaped, and liberated by the art of giving. In a way, it is like tithing but with groceries.

Giving money

It is one thing to give away some stuff that you may not use very often or refrain from purchasing more than you need. It is an entirely different thing to give away money because we can always use money. Money has become the equivalent of worth. Our language reflects this value: for instance, we talk about a person's *net worth*. How much clearer can we get? The more money you have, the more valuable you are. We have confused money with love itself.

The worship of money and the belief that money can help us solve our problems is idolatrous. If you ask people if they worship money, most will probably say no. But that's not really the truth. All of us who swim in Western culture cannot help but worship money. Money represents security and control and success. With money, I can fly anywhere in the world and get people to do almost anything for me. Without money, I have no power or influence. Without money, it seems our very lives are at risk.

There is no denying that money is an instrument of power and prestige in our world. And yet, if we worship money, it becomes our master. We will find ourselves incessantly checking our bank accounts, storing up for retirement, and working so hard that we do not enjoy life. We hoard money and hide it. We dare not speak of our salaries in this money-worshipping culture. It's ironic that a person will describe their intricate abdominal surgery to me but will not divulge how much money they earn. Somehow, we've made money sacrosanct, and secrecy around money—how much we have, how much we make—becomes a currency in and of itself. We fear that if others know the truth, they will try to find a way to take our money, to take what we believe is rightfully ours.

And this belief is reinforced at every turn. People try to hack into our bank accounts to take our money. We get emails and telephone calls from people trying to trick us into giving them access to our money. We are trained to guard our money with all our strength. We truly believe that we need money to survive. And it is true. We couldn't live without money. And yet Jesus calls us to a different way. How do we even begin?

The easiest way to write God into your budget. Begin by setting aside a small portion of your salary to give away. This doesn't have to be a large amount at first, but it should be deliberate and intentional. Pray about it. Start gently. And again, just like with prayer and worship, let go of any shame and guilt that may arise. Love yourself and celebrate the fact that you have begun a journey toward giving.

Once you determine an amount, build the timing of the gift into your regular routine. Attend church and put an envelope in the plate. Go online once a month and make a gift. Some of my parishioners set up a direct draft with the bank. While some give annually, I find this practice limits the joy as the gift is only seldom given. Even if the amount is the same, dividing it into weekly or monthly gifts helps you develop the spiritual practice of giving. At first, you may find that your mind wrestles with you when you give, but over time, a deep joy will emerge and grow.

Next you will come to the joyful but very difficult decision of where to give. It used to be that Christians gave all their gifts to the church, and the church started hospitals, housing, soup kitchens and other ministries. Today many such organizations operate separately from the church. Often, these nonprofits were born from ministries in church, but to increase their reach, they have expanded far beyond the walls of the church. For instance, the cathedral I serve has birthed six large nonprofits, focusing on issues of affordable housing, healthcare, and urban development. These nonprofits accomplish far more today than they did when they were confined to the church.

When people give today, they are encouraged to give to the church but also to give directly to the ministries that inspire them. Some choose to give to Greenpeace, some to Habitat for Humanity and so on. Others feel that it is overwhelming to give to outside causes so they give their entire gift to the church, trusting that we will birth more projects as we worship and pray and serve. The discernment process is part of the journey. It may be difficult at first but quickly becomes joyful and life-giving. And the more you give, the more you will want to give, for it anchors you spiritually in ways that are beyond words. Essentially, you are beginning to fulfill your own true nature.

Make a list of causes that seem to come from God. Look them over. Where is God calling you to give? What would it look like if you began to work toward giving 10 percent of your income for those things that are of God? Could you begin with 1 percent? Try to give before you do anything else in your budget. Write generosity into your finances, for it is essential to nurture your spiritual health.

Legacy gift

One of the greatest ways to love is to learn how to say goodbye through giving. It is ironic that departing can be loving, but it can be. At the end of life, we must give our lives away. I have witnessed the pain and even agony of families whose loved one has not made a will or a plan for dying, and I see the love that flourishes when a person loves enough to plan.

In our culture, death is equated with failure. The medical community is shaped by insurance and the fear of lawsuits. We either "save lives," or we "lose lives." This implies that when someone dies, we have lost. But death is not a failure; it is part of life. Death is unavoidable. The death rate is 100 percent. No human being has ever lived forever. It does not work that way—no matter how much Oil of Olay and other anti-aging potions you use.

Jesus died in front of the world. He hung on a cross for all to see. Artists and iconographers have tried to depict his death for millennia. Why did the incarnation of God die so publicly? Certainly, this had to happen to prepare the way for Jesus's resurrection and the promise that death is not the end but merely a doorway to eternal life. But I also believe his very public death is a poignant reminder that we too will die. Jesus was fully human as well as being fully divine. And as a person, he too had to die.

Once we face the truth about death, we can learn to live life more fully. Life is a gift given to us from God. It is to be enjoyed and to cherished, but we can experience pain and heartache when we cling too hard to life. As it says in Ecclesiastes 3:1-2a, "For everything there is a season, and a time for every matter under heaven: a time to be born, and a time to die."

But in the context of our discussion about the vital signs of the spiritual life, what does dying have to do with giving? Everything.

I have sat with many families who are grieving. I have planned many funerals. When a person has made plans for their service and when they have given away their money and belongings, the grief the family feels is still there but it is sweetened by love. The person knew they were going to die. They made plans for this day. They are giving generously so that their loved ones may live life more fully. The deceased is essentially sending this message: "I knew that this day would come, and I got ready for it. It is not your fault. I am giving to you so that you may live. I love you." To give a legacy gift is to continue to love actively even after you die. A thoughtful will can be a love letter to the world, using your life and your belongings to write the story.

Gifts left in a last will and testament have weight. They speak volumes. Think about what you want to say to the people you love. Write letters. Leave paintings, jewelry, your stamp collection, your car. And most of all, leave your money. Shockingly, in 2021, a Gallup poll found that "slightly less than half of US adults, 46%, have a will that describes how they would like their money and estate to be handled after their death. The results have been similar in three other readings on this question since 1990." Why do people not specify where their money and belongings will go after they die? Because they don't want to face the truth about death, they found it easier to avoid the subject. But in avoiding the drafting of a will, they lose out on a great opportunity to love.

If only people would be conscious and wise with their legacies, we could do so much good in the world. What causes inspire you? What keeps you up at night? Leave money in your will for them. Let it be known that you care. Let your love live on even after you die.

Jesus died in such a way that joy and new life are born. We can do the same by giving our whole lives away at the end and leaving a legacy of love behind.

Have you written a will? Begin by going online to do some research. Write down your thoughts. What would you like to give to your loved ones? What causes do you love? Think of your will as a love letter and just write it down! Don't be too critical or agonize too much. Any act of conscious legacy giving is by far better than none, no matter what you give to whom. As you go about this process, remember that you are taking a courageous step in making these decisions.

Giving to the earth

It has become painfully evident to most people that we are on a path to deplete much of the world's resources, and our waste is beginning to overwhelm the planet. Our oceans are full of plastics. More than 1,000 manatees died of starvation here in Florida in 2021 because the human population killed their plant food source through pollution. The increase of the human population has led to massive deforestation, loss of biodiversity, the degradation of land and pollution. We are literally eating our own planet alive.

The rapid pace of our consumption can overwhelm us. Where do we begin? I drive down the street on the days when the garbage is collected, and I see people throwing out incredible amounts of plastics, furniture, glass. There is just so much excess. It feels impossible to know where to begin to address the problem. How do we even take the first step? To right this incredible system of sinful consumption, we must map a way forward. We must take the first step.

The University of Florida School of Architecture created a new kind of training for architects about a decade ago. They developed a master's program called CityLab. The program is based on the premise that architects should be trained in the natural environment in which they plan to build. The first CityLab was founded in Orlando, where the students study amusement and entertainment architecture, focusing specifically on Disney World. Our cathedral has been talking with the University of Florida so that we may host another CityLab here in Jacksonville. This JaxLab, as it will be called, will be a master's level program in architecture that focuses on sustainable architecture and specifically how to build in relationship to a river, since we boast an enormous and beautiful river, the St. John's River, that runs into the sea. The program will be housed on our campus. Students of architecture will learn not only about sustainability but also hydro-generated urbanism—harnessing water for energy and regeneration—and generative design.

I come at this field as a total amateur but the idea that buildings can sustain and even enhance the environment fills me with excitement. Evidently, it is possible for us not only to reduce our consumption but also to give back, to create buildings with live plants on them, buildings that engage and sustain the earth's resources rather than deplete them. The human species does not have to damage the planet simply because we are here. We can heal the wounds we have created. We can rebuild. We can save and preserve, and we can alter our consumption.

I believe we are on the verge of discovering ways to live that have not been considered before. As Christians, we are called to watch and learn, to be flexible and willing to not only reduce our consumption but also to explore and welcome new ways of giving back. This conversation is just beginning. It will require creativity and adaptability, but we could be embarking on a joyful, new kind of living on this planet as we begin to acknowledge the dependence we have on the earth and its resources.

Consider giving not just to people but giving to nature. We can give to nonprofits that assist in caring for animals or rebuilding the forests. We can plant trees. We can give by refraining from driving whenever possible. Sometimes giving takes the form of simply not consuming. We can choose to hold back from gratifying our every desire and consider the impact of our actions on the earth first. We can live in relationship with nature and care for her as we would care for someone that we love, giving and receiving in return.

Begin with what you purchase. Before you buy anything at all, ask yourself about the impact this purchase may have on the environment. Do you need this item? Is it made of plastic? Is it biodegradable? Where will you store it? Consider buying clothing at stores that sell gently used clothing. The clothing industry alone is a major contributor to pollution.

Invest in environmentally sound companies. Choose mutual funds with these values in mind. Even burial can be a chance to give back, as you can have your body cremated and planted under a new tree. Why bury our organic bodies in cement boxes that take up space underground? Why not simply return to the dust? In this way, your death can be an opportunity to give back to the earth.

The main thing is to become conscious about our decisions and actions. Our lives belong to the earth. Let us live in ways that nourish our planet and not deplete its resources.

For Practice

Do you recycle? If not, start there. Could you plant a tree? Could you support an environmental cause? Consider what kind of practices you could begin that might nourish and even give back to the earth. Consider how you can replenish the earth with your time, your physical exertion, or your monetary gifts. Drive less whenever possible. Walk. Ride a bike. Combine your errands into one trip. Carpool.

Consider your consumption of meats and other items that deplete the earth's resources. Can you give by consuming less or even none of these things? The ideas are endless. Just take the first step.

Debt as modern-day bondage

About nine years ago, I hired an Egyptian priest to serve on our staff. Fr. Raja, his wife, Lily, and two college-age sons moved to Florida to begin a new life here with us.

Raja and Lily began a vital ministry to the immigrants and refugees that poured into Florida during this time. Because they spoke Arabic, Raja and Lily were able to communicate directly with many of the immigrants, especially those from Sudan and the Middle East. Many of the immigrants were Christian and blessed us by joining our congregation. Muslims came too, and we assisted all with ESOL (English for Speakers of Other Languages) classes, advice, relief, and job counseling.

As this ministry grew, we began to realize that many of our friends were victims of credit card debt. Not understanding English well or the American concept of the credit card, many were enticed by the lure of $15,000 in credit. They bought furniture, clothing, and other material goods with credit cards; sometimes, they even paid tuition on them. And then, the debt would mount, with credit card companies charging 15, 20, and 30-percent interest. Their debt grew worse and worse, and families began to panic. They were in a deep hole, with no idea how to dig themselves out.

I also see this happen with funeral home and death services. I see poor families encouraged to purchase fancy caskets and burial plots, using credit cards for payment. They feel obliged to spend all that they can on a fancy funeral and end up enslaved by debt in a way that their loved ones would never want.

There is no describing the panic and paralysis felt by a person who realizes that their debt is mounting faster than they can pay it off. It is a modern-day form of enslavement. And of course, the debt problem is widespread, not only encountered by immigrants but millions of people from all walks of life.

Debt is present as a concept in the Bible. It is clear as early on as the Torah that Israel understood the reality of debt and its consequences. Among the many instructions and commandments in the Book of Leviticus, God instructs the Israelites not to charge interest when loaning to a person who is poor (Leviticus 25:35-37). God also empowers the people to enjoy a jubilee year. The name jubilee derives from the Hebrew word *jobel*, which means "ram's horn." In the fiftieth year, all debts would be forgiven, all slaves freed, and people return to the land of their birth and to their families (Leviticus 25:8-10). Thus the Lord anticipated the bondage of debt and made sure that people would be given a period of grace and forgiveness, to start anew.

Jesus calls upon his followers not to charge others interest or gain by loaning out money. He instructs: "Lend, expecting nothing in return, and your reward will be great, and you will be sons of the Most High" (Luke 6:35).

As followers of Jesus, it is our vocation and ministry to assist, educate, and inform those who are caught in the trap of debt. I believe churches must educate our parishioners about the fast cash places, about funeral homes that put people in debt when they are struggling to bury a loved one. We must help people navigate the confusing morass of forms, labyrinthine lines at assistance offices, and the myriad other ways that our government programs, nonprofits, and businesses—even well-meaning ones— can overwhelm and frighten. We must walk alongside the vulnerable and equip them so that they don't find themselves drowning in debts that they cannot repay.

For Practice

Begin by making sure that you have a plan to end your own debt. If this overwhelms you, seek help from a financial adviser or a friend that you trust and make a plan. If you are debt-free, can you share your wisdom with others? Would you be able to advocate for a refugee? Could you assist others by training teenagers in the dangers of the credit card? How can you help others avoid the modern-day slavery that is debt?

Sacrificial giving

The highest form of giving is sometimes referred to as sacrifice. The word *sacrificio* in Latin literally means doing holy things (*sacra* is holy, *facere* means to do). In scripture, a sacrifice implies that a person is going to give up something, to present it at the altar. At that time, sacrifices were often an animal, a costly—and sacrificial—offering. The root of the word *sacra* implies setting something apart, removing it from its ordinary function. To sacrifice something is to set this thing aside for God and God alone. The offering is removed from this world and placed in the realm of the holy. To sacrifice means to let go of the thing here so that it may be received there. A holy gift.

In his letter to the Romans, Paul writes that we should make ourselves into a living sacrifice. He writes, "I appeal to you therefore, brothers and sisters, by the mercies of God, to present your bodies as a living sacrifice, holy and acceptable to God, which is your spiritual worship" (Romans 12:1).

What exactly is Paul trying to say? Does he mean we should all be ordained priests or become nuns and monks? I don't think he is talking about ordination at all. I think he is calling for us to give our very selves to God—about leaving this world and setting ourselves apart through our gifts.

Eventually, if you practice giving money and time, you begin to see that the most joyful times in our lives are those when we let God take charge of something, when we give ourselves fully to love, or laugh, or just really listen.

These are the times when we are able, even if just for a few moments, to lose ourselves in art or writing or speaking or in a science project or math problem. For a few moments, we are one with our Maker, and all is well. It is not a bloody sacrifice or even painful, but it is sacrifice, for in that sacred moment, we move aside and let God take us and set us apart.

What is sacrifice? It is the holy giving that sets the self aside, not out of self-debasement or self-abandonment but out of the simple clarity that God is in control, and it is time for us to step out of the driver's seat.

Sacrifice is counter-intuitive and countercultural. It goes against everything Americans have been trained to believe and to practice. We are told every day, multiple times a day, to consume, purchase, and make decisions for ourselves. To sacrifice is to set ourselves aside and instead refrain from consumption and give instead. Is this hard? Most of the time, yes. Will it be painful? Sometimes, yes. Is it worth it? Yes.

Remember: the big lie of consumerism is that you will be happy if you take. This ancient lie began with the serpent in the Garden of Eden. Things will be better if you take, if you possess, if you own, the serpent promised. But this was a lie then, and it's a lie now. There is no material thing that you can take that will make you happy. It is actually better if you give.

Saint Paul practices the act of *kenosis* or self-emptying. Other saints in the church have as well. But so too have ordinary people who have an extraordinary capacity for giving. This practice of *kenosis* can lead to poverty and, for a few, even martyrdom. Joyfully giving up everything for God is the highest level of Christian giving, and it can only be accomplished by those steeped in prayer and in worship. It is a vision for us to strive toward, something for us to hope to attain one day. It is the way of Jesus himself.

For Practice

How can you give enough so that you are experiencing that place of self-emptying? Go to the edge of your capacity, but make sure you are giving with joy. Find your balance and be kind to yourself.

Finding your way to give

Just as the pulse pumps blood through the body, so giving brings life to our spiritual lives. Giving pours love into the world, and its activity is easily measured. Giving is a concrete way of sharing the gift of life with the rest of the world. It is, at its heart, our way of acting like Jesus, who gave everything to us. You can assess this vital sign of the spiritual life by looking at your budget and by measuring the time that you give. Is God high on your priority list? Is your money given to things that edify others, the natural world, your community of faith? How often do you give and how much? After I jog, I like to check and see that my pulse is faster. Can you raise your pulse, your giving, so that you might develop strength and new life? It is never too late to examine our giving and to challenge ourselves to give more.

ETERNAL GOD, *you are always giving, always creating and reaching out to us in love. Guide us to learn the deep truth of our existence, that, as your Son Jesus so simply said, "It is more blessed to give than to receive." Show us how to give with joy and gladness so that we may become more like you, and so that our love for you may flow freely now and always. In Christ's abundant love, we pray. Amen.*

Grow
The Temperature

Repent! For the kingdom of heaven is at hand.
—Matthew 4:17b

If change and growth are not *programmed into* your spirituality, if there are not serious warnings about the blinding nature of fear and fanaticism, your religion will *always* end up worshipping the status quo and protecting your present ego position and personal advantage—as if it were God!
—Richard Rohr, *Falling Upward*

The human body is in constant motion. The speed of this motion and the level of exertion creates a temperature, hot or cold. A fever, or elevated body temperature, is a sign the body is fighting infection, and the activity going on inside the body—the motion and exertion involved in the fight— is generating too much heat. While the body is always in motion and generating heat, we don't want the cells of the body to move too fast or fight too hard; this type of extreme activity can put the body at risk. On the flip side, when a body becomes too cold, the cells slow down their motion, creating hypothermia and even death.

The material world is always moving and changing. Plants spring new roots, and trees die and decay. Animals give birth, and mountains erode. Children grow. Elders age. Hair changes color and texture. Skin changes according to wind and weather. There is no stasis in the physical world.

The same is true in the spiritual world, both here and in the heavenly realms. Change is the one constant. We know our spiritual lives in this world are ever changing, but I believe our spiritual lives in heaven will also be moving and changing. Some have an image of heaven as stagnant—a place where people sit on white clouds in heaven playing harps and nothing ever changes. This image gives us the impression that the goal of salvation is to remain the same and that heaven is a place where things never change. Nothing could be further from the truth. Jesus says we have been given eternal life, and since life means growth and change, eternal life must mean eternal growth and eternal change. There is nothing boring or stagnant about that!

In our physical world today, fear is a driving force for us to resist change and growth. We are innately afraid of the unknown—and change is a direct encounter with the unknown. This primal part of our nature makes sense.

As children, we are comforted and even strengthened by stability and predictability. We like to surround ourselves with known quantities—people, jobs, activities. We delight in the familiar.

Even though stability comforts us, this world, in both its physical and spiritual aspects, is constantly changing. The planet rotates on its axis. The cells of our body grow and die. There is no holding still in this world. If we do not take on growth as an opportunity, then we will keep moving, but we will move backward and not forward. Staying the same means regressing. People age: material objects wear out and crumble. Even when we try to remain the same, the world moves out from under us.

Metanoia

When I lived in Connecticut many years ago, I moved in across the street from a very old woman. She kept all her curtains closed. Her bushes grew up to block the light from shining into her windows. I knocked on her door to introduce myself, and when she opened the door, I could see that she had a large, infected wound on her calf. Her house dress was dirty, and a stench wafted from the front hall. I asked if she was ok. She said yes and closed the door quickly. This woman was trying to block out the world.

For the next few weeks, I continued to knock on her door every few days, and she continued to make excuses. Meanwhile, her leg grew redder and more swollen and began to ooze fluid. Finally, I got scared and called a social worker, who admitted her to the hospital. After rehabilitation, she returned home, but this time, she refused to open her door. Months later, the mailman called the police when her mail backed up. She had died alone on her kitchen floor.

This woman tried to keep change at bay. She tried her best to stay the same. She locked her doors and closed her curtains. She wanted to halt time itself, but it didn't work. She died alone because she was frightened to live. In her fear, she ended up making the biggest change—from living to dying—all alone.

To live is to change and grow. So long as we are alive, we will change. The question is: will we fight the change or lean into it? Will we shut the door and lock it, or will we open the door to growth?

God presents us the opportunity to grow each moment of our lives. We are given a chance to learn from everything, from the dandelion that blows in the wind to a car that cuts us off in traffic. We can learn from every experience: the good, the bad, and the ugly. And, in a case of irony, we tend to learn the most when we fail and suffer. Often, discomfort, fear, and even pain can spur the best kind of growth. Herein lies one of the many dimensions of the mystery of the cross.

When Jesus tells everyone to repent in the Gospel of Matthew, the word he uses is *metanoia*. *Metanoia* literally means to turn outward to God, to turn away from the self and to the Almighty. *Metanoia* is the opposite of paranoia, which means to turn into the self in fear. Just like the earth rotates, we are constantly turning; the question is, which way will we turn? To the self or to God? This is the fundamental choice of each human being: Who will I serve? Toward whom will I move?

It honors God when we seek to learn about this world in all its aspects. All forms of education and learning, at their best, involve a curiosity, an interest, the giving of our attention to this world. To be fascinated with the world in any aspect is to do it honor, to acknowledge that God's creation possesses innate wisdom and can become our teacher. God wants us to observe the creation that has been made, to marvel at it and study it and stand in awe of it. God made us for this.

For Practice

What does it mean to you that you are constantly changing and growing? Do you embrace this idea or approach it with fear and trembling? What steps can you take to practice metanoia, of turning away from self and toward God?

Seeking knowledge

In her insightful book, *The Color Purple*, Alice Walker writes of Shug, a beautiful nightclub singer who expresses her understanding of God in this way, "I think that it pisses God off if you pass by the color purple in a field and don't notice it..." In other words, God is showing off for us! Like a playful child, God essentially says, "Here! Look at what I just made! Isn't it beautiful? Look at the intricacies of the atom, the magnificence of a quark, the speed of light, the complexity of the human mind, the glory of a sonata, the luminosity of the moon. Don't waste your life trying to fix yourself or being obsessed with yourself. You were not designed to look at yourself. Instead, look outward and see the wondrous works!"

Some people seek and absorb knowledge across a wide arena. They are collectors of information, spurred by curiosity to learn and grow in many areas. Others may be drawn into a deep dive into a particular discipline. Think of people who study for years to understand how diamonds are formed or who are so awestruck by jazz that they spend their lives trying to play. Mathematicians seek to find solutions, historians to remember the past and learn from it. Scientists study the workings of the physical world, while writers seek to describe it. These are people keen on exploring the world, learning to listen and observe, committed to growth. They relate to the world with fascination, respect, and awe. They invite the created order to teach them—an acknowledgment that this same order possesses a wisdom worth understanding. This way of learning and growing is an act of devotion.

The same is true of our spiritual lives. When we approach our relationship with God with curiosity, fascination, respect, and awe, we will want to learn. We will seek opportunities to listen and observe. We will look for ways to deepen our knowledge and expand our horizons. To do otherwise is turn our backs on the wisdom and love of God. Spiritual health requires growth—some painful, some joyful, all in the pursuit of a deeper relationship with God.

What fascinates you? What do you yearn to learn more about? Now that we have access to technology, there is no stopping you from learning all about those areas in which God speaks to you. Indulge your intellectual curiosity and devote some time to nourishing your growth.

About the Bible

> The word is very near you, it is in your mouth and in your heart for you to observe.
>
> —Deuteronomy 30:14

It sounds so obvious that I recommend you read the Bible. Of course. I'm a priest. I would say that. A doctor may be able to tell that you have a fever by holding a hand to your forehead, but a thermometer is a much better tool for diagnosis and next steps. In the same way, reading the Bible truly is one of the best ways to grow. There is no substitute.

In the ordination vows, priests in the Episcopal Church state that they believe, "the Bible to be the Word of God and to contain all things necessary to salvation." You may wonder: why do priests have to take this vow? This is because the Bible is fundamental to who we are as Christians.

Let's back up a bit first. I want to be clear: when we say that the Bible is the Word of God, we do not mean that a holy pen came down from heaven to write all the words.

We mean that God inspired people to write it—all different kinds of people over hundreds and hundreds of years. At first, these sacred stories were passed verbally. Devout people memorized them, a practice that many religions still adhere to today. At some point, people began to write down these recitations. The first texts were scrolls, and they were made in such a way that you could add swaths of scroll: the ancients did not believe the scripture was ever really finished, that God could always add more. It wasn't until the fourth century after Christ's birth that the church "canonized" the Bible. In canonizing the Bible, scholars of the day determined which books were in and which were out. So, you may hear people talk about non-canonical books, other early Christian documents that may provide interesting context but are not part of the New Testament canon.

Even the word "book" of the Bible as a concept developed later in Christian history. When these sacred stories were first being written down, there was no such thing as a book, not in the way that we understand it today. No one produced a piece of writing that existed between two covers with a beginning and an end. In fact, the closest Hebrew word we have to the word for book is *sefer*, which can best be translated as something recounted, or another translation might be scroll. A scroll was not some writing shut in between two covers; there was an open-ended quality to the writing, the idea that the stories of God were ongoing and always open to additions.

Authorship was also different than we view it today. It didn't matter so much about who wrote the words as what they said. Indeed, authorship wasn't even considered important until the time of the prophets. In fact, scholars today still are conflicted about the authors for some of the books of the Bible. For instance, there are different strands of authorship in the book of Genesis and in the Torah, the first five books of the Bible. Different writers refer to God by different names, some using the name *Yahweh* for God or the name *Elohim*. As Robert Alter, a professor of Hebrew, writes, "Enormous energy has been invested in discriminating the precise boundaries between one document and the next." And yet, the Bible that has come to us is a beautiful and coherent piece of artistry. I like to think of it as a mosaic or tapestry, the myriad authors and voices like threads woven together to create a piece of extraordinary beauty. Some see the Bible as a choir of many voices that produces an other-worldly sound, or as Alter describes, "other works of art that evolve over the centuries, like the cathedrals of medieval Europe, and are the product of many hands." Regardless of which metaphor we use, it's undeniable that the Bible is a work of art, shaped by God through the audial and then literary voices of people who told an ancient story. And as a work of art, it must be approached not just with the intellect but with the heart. It must be absorbed and felt and sensed.

As you read and study the Bible, it's also important to consider the ancient languages and the limits of accurate translation. The Old Testament is written in Hebrew. The

New Testament was written in *koine* Greek, (with *koine* meaning common). These ancient languages had far fewer words that we do in modern English. So, even in translating a single word from Hebrew or Greek, we are taking an ancient word with all kinds of meanings and dimensions and translating it into, on average, 14-17 very precise English words. Inevitably, the meaning changes. To bring scripture into the vernacular is to shape and influence its meaning, to make choices and to drive it into a limited sphere. That is why many Muslims simply refuse to translate the Quran because they know the difficulties. To translate is to limit and to interpret. We must always keep this in mind. This is why Bible study in community is so essential. When you struggle with the meaning of a verse in the Bible, don't just write it off or complain. Instead, go deeper! Examine the roots of the language. With the internet, language translation is so much more accessible, even to those who have absolutely no foundation in the ancient language. So don't stop digging and unearthing. Exploring these ancient scriptures is a bit like archaeology: we must dig deep to plumb the depths of its meaning.

We've compared the Bible to encountering art and going on an archaeological dig, but the most important aspect of the sacred text is that it is alive. When we say that the Bible is the Word of God, we are saying that the Spirit of God moves in and through it. To read the Bible is to enter into a relationship with it. And this relationship, like all relationships, will change you. Like any relationship, reading the Bible takes time, and it takes commitment.

For Practice

Begin by simply opening the Bible once a day. There are new apps for your smart phones that can send you a single verse daily. Start with small but daily bites.

Reading the Bible

The American mind is very different today than it was even a decade ago. The way we receive information is different, and it's affected our attention spans and ability to focus. Many of us struggle if we sit down and try to read long passages of scripture. The mind wanders, creating diversions and producing a sense of guilt and frustration. Given this, my recommendation is to take small bites. Approach the sacred scripture in small amounts that you can hear or digest.

Even in Jesus's day, attention spans tended to be short. That's why Jesus used short parables or stories to convey powerful messages about God's love and desires for us. Jesus drew on familiar imagery and contexts, often from nature or farming. Even though these parables were short, they weren't simple! In fact, so much meaning is packed into these small passages that you could meditate on one for a year and not find an end to its meaning. Desert Fathers in the sixth and seventh centuries locked themselves in caves with just one parable, and when they emerged some time later, claimed that they still couldn't plumb the depths of its meaning. All this is to say that taking small bites of scripture isn't giving the Bible short shrift. In fact, I think the shortness of the passages enables us to go deeper and to be fed more profoundly.

In my personal experience, I have found that reading small passages of scripture each day has a deeper impact both on my knowledge of the text and my ability to grow spiritually. Just as we must exercise the body daily in reasonable amounts that push but do not injure or overtax the system, so too the reading of scripture must be taken daily in reasonable amounts. It is the practice of daily meditation on the text that enables the words to sink deeply into the soul. Don't think about how much scripture you consume all at once; rather, try to partake in it daily in an amount that you can retain.

For Practice

Take small bites of scripture daily. Here are some ways to get started:

1. I host a 5-minute daily Bible devotion each morning. It can be accessed on YouTube (search for my name). This could be a good way for you to begin this healthy habit.

2. Another way is to follow the instructions in the section at the end of the Book of Common Prayer called the Daily Office. If you follow the Daily Office, you'll read a small section of scripture each day. Depending on how much you choose to read each day, you can end up reading the entire Bible in the course of two, four, or six years.

3. Join a simple Bible study. This is a good start, especially for those who are more extroverted. You don't need an ordained, seminary-trained leader (although those types of studies can be helpful too!) Simply gather a group, agree on what you will read each week, and then discuss your reflections on the readings.

4. The Bible Challenge is another excellent resource. This series, published by Forward Movement, lays out reading plans and reflections for reading the entire Bible in a year, particular books of the Bible over 40 or 50 days, or a topical reading plan (such as social justice or creation care). Visit ForwardMovement.org to learn more.

Taking in the news

A couple from my parish decided to go on a six-week hiking and camping trip from late August to mid-October in 2001. They were in the woods on September 11 when the planes hit the Twin Towers in New York City. They met someone who told them what had happened, so they found their way into a small town where they sat at a bar and watched the news for about an hour. Then they went back to the woods.

My friends were, of course, concerned, and they prayed for this country and for the world, but they continued their trip until its scheduled end.

When they returned home, my friends realized that the rest of this country had suffered from trauma. Their neighbors, relatives, and friends had all been affected profoundly by the horror of the event and by the sight of people jumping out of windows to their death, images that replayed repeatedly on the television and internet. People were frightened, and they were angry.

My friends were grateful they had been in the woods—they had been buffered from the atrocity by the beauty of nature, the calm voice of the wind in the trees. The terror attacks did not hit them as close to home. Their brains did not possess running tapes of horror.

How can we grow and develop our compassion and wisdom in a world where we cannot think straight? How can we listen to God when our lives are so noisy and busy that we can't remember the last time we sat in silence? How can we discern our call from God—take our spiritual temperature, if you will—when we can't even absorb what's going on around us?

Our 24-hour news cycle seems to feed on crisis and despair. If this is all we see and read, then it would be easy to think that the world is on the brink of catastrophe—all the time! We know in our heads and hearts that there is much good that transpires, but good news rarely sells. If we're not careful, we can find ourselves on a merry-go-round of fear and anxiety, upheaval and discord.

Let me be clear: I believe it is important for every person to be aware of what is transpiring in the world. We should not hide. We must know the truth about the state of our world, and we are called to pray for everything. But we must create a container within which we can digest this material. We cannot continue to drink from a firehose of nonstop news. To develop our spiritual lives and indeed our character, we must know how to take in this information—and how to turn off the spigot.

Most of us agree about the importance of protecting our children from excessive media and technology. But we do not recognize that we also need to protect ourselves. We must take charge of our own attention, setting guidelines and limits so that we control when and how we engage with the headlines.

But how do you determine how much media to digest? What is the right balance for you? That is something that I cannot tell you. You must find your sweet spot, a way to keep you both informed and able to reflect. I tend to watch less news programs and instead read more newspapers. I find the written word is easier to absorb. I read *The New York Times*, the *Wall Street Journal*, and the local paper, all as best as I can. I am also on social media, mainly to keep in touch with my family, friends, and the needs of my parishioners. Still, I try to limit my time on social media, knowing I can't possibly keep up with every post from every friend.

I also am a dinosaur trying to navigate a technological world that I was not born into. Unlike younger generations who are digital natives, I am a digital immigrant, and as such, I will never feel completely at home in it. Technology can be an incredible tool, and I am grateful for its arrival, but I also realize that it is my responsibility to provide healthy parameters for use. This kind of self-protection and discipline is essential to the life of the spirit and the healthy growth of a human being.

For Practice

Reflect on how you can best digest the news without overwhelming yourself. Can you read a paper daily or two? Can you listen to a daily news podcast (maybe in the car)? Do you like to sit in front of the TV to take in the news? Take charge of the way you ingest the news and triage your input so that you remain healthy and objective.

Mysterious pace of growth

Other seeds fell on rocky ground, where they did not have much soil, and they sprang up quickly, since they had no depth of soil. —Matthew 13:5

Most people think growth should happen quickly. We live, after all, in the culture of the quick fix. But despite our desire to get change done quickly, most significant and permanent change often happens gradually, and people who race to grow often wither or withdraw. When someone tries to lose weight rapidly, for example, they often gain that weight right back again, whereas those who diet slowly and with care often keep the weight off.

Do not think of growth as something that is at its essence results oriented. Think instead of the journey of learning and changing as part of the essence of who we are as human beings. We were made in the image of God, and God is ever changing and growing, moving and dancing.

Rapid change can be especially damaging when it comes to institutions and systems. There are times when an awakening to justice mandates rapid change, but this change often happens at a cost, as people are left behind and cannot accept the transition.

I have learned over the years that my congregation can manage incredible adaptive change if it is done gradually and with much education and discussion. People are willing to manage transitions when they feel that they have a voice, even if that voice is not the final word. Giving people information as to why a change is being considered, giving warning and a waiting period before the change, and providing the gift of being heard help smooth the transition of change and are essential steps for effective leaders.

After all, if we move ahead, but no one follows, are we actually leading?

I recently visited the lighthouse on Cape Hatteras in the Outer Banks of North Carolina. This lighthouse stands 210 feet high and is the tallest brick lighthouse structure in the United States—and the second tallest in the world. In 1999, engineers realized the lighthouse had to be moved because the sea was encroaching, and the shore was eroding. If it wasn't moved, the lighthouse was just 15 feet from the ocean and would certainly be swept into the sea. Change of some sort was inevitable.

The plan to move the lighthouse was controversial. Many thought such a move would permanently damage or even destroy the lighthouse. Lawsuits were filed and later dismissed. Ultimately, the International Chimney and Expert House Movers dug a track beneath the lighthouse and then extended the same track all the way to a new location 2,900 feet inland. It took them 23 days to move the lighthouse 2,900 feet because they moved so slowly. But their care and deliberation paid off. The lighthouse was moved without suffering any damage at all—and the team even won an award for outstanding achievement in civil engineering! The lighthouse was moved successfully because of one thing: they did it slowly and deliberately.

As you examine your spiritual life and consider changes you want to make to strengthen it, remember the story of the Cape Hatteras Lighthouse and take things one small step at a time. Remember that gradual change is often much more effective and stronger than rapid change. Develop spiritual practices of scripture reading, prayer, gratitude, and giving that you can commit to and sustain. Take them one small step at a time. Be patient. Remember: Rome was not built in a day, and the lighthouse took nearly a month to move!

For Practice

Is there someone in your life who you wish would grow faster or come to see the light as you do? Give them the gift of space and time. Practice gentleness and humbleness of heart while still calling them forward in growth.

Your passion

Craig Minor was a member of my parish in Wichita, Kansas. He was a professor and a true historian. Craig approached the study of history like a child in a candy shop. He was absolutely fascinated by everything that had transpired in the past and by what these stories could teach us about our present reality. Craig was particularly driven to write the history of his beloved home state, Kansas.

Craig helped me plan Bible study and formation classes for adults. We would meet frequently at a local coffee shop where his joy was palpable. "We should study this!" he would exclaim. Or "Have you read this book?" His long, gangly legs didn't fit under our small, cramped table, but his smile filled the room.

As a result of his joy in learning, Craig was bitten by the writing bug. He wrote book after book. They just seemed to flow out of him. It was a never-ending stream. He was a man who had found his passion, and in doing so, his work became his worship.

How can you find your passion? First, spend timing honestly assessing and asking questions: What type of learning captivates you? Where do you naturally gravitate when you have free time and are not exhausted? What sites do you visit on the internet? What books do you pick off the shelves? What lessons do you long to learn?

Finding your passion for growth and learning is a lot like identifying your favorite foods. Don't be shy. Are you fascinated with people and their dynamics? Do you love fashion? Hospitality? Cooking? Blowing glass? There should be no judgment and no shame in finding your passion. There is no right and wrong.

Find the places that ignite, engage, inspire you. Go where the Spirit leads you and nowhere else.

Let curiosity and pure joy drive you to find your passions.
This search should be an adventure that produces energy
and enthusiasm. If it becomes drudgery or depressing, take
a step back and ask yourself when and where you lost your
joy. Go back there and retrace your steps. Don't stop until
you find the place where you encounter new life, and then
begin anew.

Suffering

In her book, *Belonging: Remembering Ourselves Home*,
Toko-pa Turner writes about suffering and struggle:

> What if [suffering and negative emotions] have
> something essential to communicate to us and each
> other, and the real problem is that misguided attitude
> that negative feelings make us less evolved and need
> fixing? In the same way that we hold others at an
> arm's length when they are too different from us, we
> avoid the inner encounter with otherness, excluding
> anything that doesn't fit the image we've been
> building of ourselves.

One of the greatest teachers in this life is pain. When we
feel pain, we learn that something is not working the way it
is supposed to. Pain is a catalyst for change and growth.

When I am in bed at night, I will lie in one position for a good long time sleeping. But at some time in the night, my body sends a message to my brain that I am no longer comfortable in this position. Without even waking up, this small amount of discomfort urges my body to roll over, to adjust the way that the body lies on the bed. This unconscious adjustment is spurred by discomfort. It prevents me from getting bedsores, kinks in my neck, and other small injuries. The discomfort causes change, and the change is good. Even in sleep, we must move and adjust.

When you experience pain in the body, it is a message from the body to the brain that something needs adjusting, healing, fixing, changing. It is nothing more than a communication, albeit an urgent one. It is a message.

When we feel emotional or psychological pain, it is also a message. Take grief for example. When a person you love dies, you grieve. Your mind and body are used to hearing this person's voice, smelling, touching, seeing them. And then they are gone. The pain you feel is your mind and body forcing itself to adjust to the absence. And it hurts like hell. This grief reveals the truth of absence and the consequences of loss. But if we allow ourselves to experience it, grief can spur us to change and grow, to explore new adventures. If we refuse to feel the grief, if we ignore it or bottle it up, or if we refuse to allow it to change us and to grow, it can sit on us like a boulder and prevent us from living fully.

Allowing suffering to teach us is difficult. Full stop. It means that we must allow ourselves to feel the suffering. We must listen to it and ask ourselves questions: Why am I in pain? Am I reliving something that I have been too afraid to confront? Am I running from a part of my past that has yet to be seen and heard by me?

I am a big proponent of therapy as a means for spiritual and psychological growth. Inviting another person to look with you at your life story is scary, but it can also set you free. It can help us break out of damaging patterns, so we don't repeat bad decisions. We do have a choice, but we cannot make that choice, we cannot be free, unless we first identify that which enslaves us.

At some point, if you are pursuing growth, you will be invited to tell the story of your life. And when you tell that story, you will be able to write the ending as well. Do you learn from your mistakes and grow from the pain that you experience? Or do you repeat the same patterns of relationships and loss? It is your choice. Once you grow enough to tell your story, you can choose how the story unfolds. You can choose how to respond to the events of your life from that point forward.

I have been blessed with a wonderful therapist. She has walked with me through some of the greatest challenges of my life and allowed me to learn from my pain. She once explained to me that many people in the world will live their entire lives repeating the same patterns and feeling the same pain without ever waking up or making the necessary changes to heal their lives. What drives some people to learn and grow while others simply survive? What drives some to seek true healing and health while others simply wallow in the same patterns? This is truly a mystery, but it lies at the heart of our spiritual lives. God calls us to do the hard work, to face our fears and change our lives, to love ourselves enough to no longer put up with abuse and situations that cause us undue anxiety or depression and other stressors. God has given every one of us the capacity to grow. The question is: will we choose to do so?

As we consider how pain can be a tool for growth, we need look no further than the cross. The fact that God decided to endure the worst kind of physical and psychological pain a human being could ever experience tells us something important. God moved through this pain, through this horror, and emerged victorious on the other side. The cross was taken on voluntarily by the Holy One who could have simply wiped out the entire planet. But instead, God chose to suffer and die for us, to experience pain and to live again. God showed us the way through pain, not around it or running from it, but through it. That is the way of the cross, the way of life and growth. That is God's gift to you and to me. Pain is not the enemy; it is a messenger. All it asks is to be heard.

*Reflect on your life and write down experiences of pain
and sorrow in a journal or other special place. Ask yourself:
What has your suffering taught you? How can your suffering
be used to the glory of God in ministry to others? In other
words, how can you lift up your cross and follow Jesus?*

Confession, Examen, and other tools

In the early 1500s, a Spanish priest by the name of Ignatius
of Loyola began to teach prayer in a new way. He called this
prayer practice the Examen. This practice asks everyone
to reflect on their actions and to learn from their mistakes.
Ignatius advised that we do this "examination" twice a day,
at noon and at bedtime. The idea is that we pause and spend
time reflecting on the events of that day. While they are
still fresh in our minds, we ask ourselves: where was God in
my day? Did I encounter God as I should? Often, I find that
when I practice the Examen, I encounter some inadequacies
or mistakes that I have made. I must then ask myself how I
can improve tomorrow. How can God help me become more
loving, more generous, more insightful than yesterday? I
experience God's forgiveness and love but also the impetus
to become more and more like Christ. In this way, the
Examen is a catalyst for growth.

Those who see themselves as perfect, as needing no
improvement, will not grow. Those who refuse to look at

themselves and examine their lives will not grow. How can we learn if we are unwilling to admit our shortcomings? How can we grow if we think we have grown enough? The key element to the Examen is the solid trust that we are human, limited in our understanding and awareness, and that God teaches us through the events of our lives and particularly through the events in which we fall short. In this light, mistakes are a gift from God, a tool for increased awareness and growth.

Most Christians in this country no longer practice regular confession. But confession is a beautiful practice. It is the ancestor of therapy. In the Episcopal Church, this practice is called reconciliation, in part because it liberates and refreshes. Acknowledging our mistakes and shortcomings gives us an opportunity to reconcile with God and others. We learn and grow from this teaching tool, and a good confessor will never condemn but instead instruct. There is no greater lesson than that which is written in the repetitive patterns of our lives. If you make the same mistakes repeatedly, God is inviting you to look at those mistakes not with guilt or shame but with curiosity and kindness. With detachment and compassion, we can look at our own actions as signals of our blind spots. And those areas in which we fail can become our greatest areas of opportunity.

For Practice

Find a priest, spiritual director, monk, or nun and try a
sacramental confession. This may be scary to contemplate,
but I guarantee you will be rewarded! You can learn more
about confession (or "The Reconciliation of a Penitent") in
the Book of Common Prayer, starting on page 447.

Saints

How monotonously alike all the great tyrants and
conquerors have been: how gloriously different are
the saints.

—C.S. Lewis, *Mere Christianity*

A few years ago, I visited Assisi, the small town in Italy
where Saint Francis lived. Saint Francis walked this earth
almost a thousand years ago, but you can feel him when you
visit Assisi. His presence is palpable. I was riveted.

Saint Francis was a rich merchant's son who gave up his
wealth to live a life of poverty and service. He was in love
with God. I say "in love" because he would go into periods
of ecstasy, during which he would sing and cry and dance
and act like a person madly in love. During a time when
the church had gone astray with wealth and corruption,
Francis called Christians back to simplicity and a life lived
in communion with nature. Francis died young, but his life
was like a stone that hits the water. The ripples of his impact

grew in strength and power. Today, millions remember and honor the life of Saint Francis, and he is one of the most beloved of all Christian saints (and the namesake of the current pope!).

Why do we need saints? In his book, *My Life with Saints*, James Martin, SJ wisely writes that saints are like our friends. We simply can't have too many of them!

> We learn by emulating others. We learn and grow when we see other human beings praying and learning and growing. We become our true selves when we have someone to compare ourselves to. And the saints are each magnificent, unique, and vibrant examples of people who found their particular path to God. They are our role models.

If you are looking to grow in your understanding and love of God, there is no better way than to learn about the life of a saint. What did they do? Why did they love God so much? How did they choose to serve God? The saints are as colorful as a rainbow, and their stories are fascinating, strange, and even crazy. There is never a dull moment with the saints. Their stories are brilliant and interesting. And we can feel them telling us, "Well, it's your turn. What crazy thing can you do for God 'with your one wild and precious life?'" (as the poet Mary Oliver so aptly put it).

Who are you? What is your path to devotion? When you learn about the saints, you hear about more options, more examples, more choices. They give us possibilities.

Through the ancient traditions of the church, we also believe we can pray to the saints and ask them to intercede for us. In other words, not only are the saints role models but also advocates, intermediaries, consultants. They can be a lifeline to Jesus, making his life and ministry more accessible to us who long to follow him. They can be our trainers as we start the hard work of growing.

Learning and growing happens when we encounter new challenges. The lives of the saints challenge us for they offer examples of people whose commitment to Jesus was extraordinary and who were willing to sacrifice many of life's comforts on the road to intimacy with God.

When you specialize in a field, you learn most from those who are experts in that field. We gain wisdom from those who are further down the road, who have worked longer, experienced more, read more, and studied more. I instruct my staff to find at least three people who are experts in their field and get them to share their insights. It is the best way to learn.

Saints are the experts in the Christian life—not that they did everything right, but they were all in, fully committed to Jesus. They made Christ their first priority, and their witness and example can help us increase our devotion and love for God.

Finding your way to growth

Just as the body temperature must be maintained and the cells must move apace, so we must engage daily in spiritual growth. The main thing is to keep open. Keep your heart open. Keep your mind open. Be willing to adapt, learn, adjust, and reconsider. Come to each day with the fresh awareness that you are simple, small, and beloved and that there is so much for you to learn. Keep moving toward knowledge, wisdom, and compassion. Growth is a never-ending movement that gives life to the soul.

When I was much younger, I knew a brilliant biologist. He once said to me that the more you know, the greater the circumference of the unknown. It is like cutting down trees in a forest: when you have only cut down three trees, the circumference of the forest is small. That is why preschoolers feel that they know everything. But the more we learn, the more we realize the incredible vastness of the universe, of all that is unknown. By the time of his death, this brilliant biologist told me that he was totally ignorant. "I stand in awe of the mysteries of the universe," he said.

Remember too that just as a plant grows in its own time and in its own way, so your spiritual growth is yours and yours alone. There is no way to compare your spiritual journey with that of another. There can be no competition in the spiritual life. It simply doesn't work. It is like trying to compare an orange to an elephant.

Growth at its heart is an act of devotion that produces both awe and humility. And it never ends, not in this life, nor God willing, in the life to come.

ALMIGHTY GOD, *you call us to grow just as you call us to live, for life is growth and it is change. Help us to lean into the movement of your living, moving Holy Spirit and to not be afraid to open our hearts and minds to new ideas, new practices, new concepts. Help us to rest in the assurance that you dance with us into newness of life each moment of each day. In Jesus's name we pray. Amen.*

Group
The Pressure

Keeping every part of the body supplied with sufficient quantities of blood at all times is a tricky business. Every time you stand up, roughly a pint and a half of your blood tries to drain downward, and your body has to somehow overcome the dead pull of gravity. To manage this, your veins contain valves that stop blood from flowing backward, and the muscles in your legs act as pumps when they contract, helping blood in the lower body get back to the heart. To contract, however, they need to be in motion. That's why it important to get up and move around regularly...As you may gather from this, blood pressure isn't a fixed figure, but changes from one part of the body to another, and across the body as a whole throughout the day.

—Bill Bryson, *The Body: A Guide for Occupants*

Blood pressure measures the movement and amount of blood in the body. It is always changing. Movement and exercise can increase blood pressure in the moment, but these healthy activities, if done regularly and consistently, can help lower blood pressure. High blood pressure, caused by lifestyle choices, genetics, or disease, can ultimately lead to serious illness and even death. A healthy blood pressure signals a balance in the body; it's a sign of wellness and vitality. The same is true of "group," the final vital sign of the spiritual life. There can be no true, sustained growth or discernment for an individual without being part of a group that gathers to pray, talk, and listen together. Balance plays a role even in the conception and practice of the group: a healthy one finds the balance of motion, between sharing and listening, meeting and giving each other space. To find your group is to find your balance in the spiritual life.

Loving relationships

By this everyone will know that you are my disciples,
if you have love for one another.
—John 13:35

When the disciples ask Jesus what they need to do to follow
him, he tells them to love one another. It sounds simple,
almost child-like. But as with much of what Jesus says, it
is both simple and, at the same time, profound beyond all
understanding.

Throughout the world, humans struggle to find a way to
relate to one another in peace. A Roman Catholic man
was killed by a mob of Protestants in Ireland a few years
ago, beaten to death for being another type of Christian.
Palestinians and Israelis hate one another with such a
vengeance that peace often seems unattainable. Terrorist
groups blow up human beings in the name of God. Humans
are killed, trafficked, defiled, and shamed. We are no better
at getting along with one another today than we were in
Jesus's day.

How do we stop fighting? How can we learn to be in
relationship with one another in ways that are not hurtful,
destructive, or fallen? How can we learn to live in love?
These age-old questions have never been answered
adequately, and I am not so deluded as to think I have finally
come up with the solution. But God has given us some
pretty darn good tools that we have not fully accessed or

understood. And I believe the most important tool is the Trinity. God has given us the revelation of the nature of God in the form of the Trinity. Some understand the Trinity as Father, Son, and Holy Spirit. Others use terms such as Creator, Redeemer, and Sanctifier. Within the concept of the Trinity is everything that we need to know about loving relationships. Within the Holy Trinity, we can find a road map to peace and understanding for the whole human race. All we need to do is look deeply into the scripture.

Let us begin with this simple and profound idea: God is relationship. Perfect, loving, divine relationship. By studying the intricacies of the relationship between God the Father, God the Son, and God the Holy Spirit, we can learn how to get along with one another. We must study the Godhead and then apply its qualities to our own lives. The Trinity gives us hope, a path to peace. Out of the chaos and darkness, we can find a way forward. Together.

For Practice

Sit in silence and ponder God as constant motion, constant relationship, constant love. Ponder all the motion of love that exists in nature and between individuals. Stand in awe of this mystery and beauty.

The myth of being alone

> Then God said, "Let us make humankind in our image,
> according to our likeness."
>
> —Genesis 1:26a

> Then the Lord God said, "It is not good the man
> should be alone."
>
> —Genesis 2:18a

It is clear from the very first words of scripture that God made humanity in the image of God. God created humankind in the image of "us." This plural pronoun makes clear that God has company within the divine self. Humanity is made in the image of a multifaceted God who has love and relationship within and without. This is one of the many passages of scripture that is used to point to the theological concept of the Trinity.

I sit on the borderline between introvert and extrovert. As dean of a cathedral, I am often surrounded by people. By the end of some days, I long to be alone. Sometimes, I rush up to the chapel on the third floor for a few precious moments of silence and then descend with eagerness to meet the next beautiful soul. Other times, I relish the frequent interactions with parishioners and community members. I love being alone, and I love being with people, but it is essential that I find a balance between the two or I can find myself overwhelmed.

Today is a rare Sabbath Saturday. I am home alone. My kids are all busy and out. I have an entire day to myself. I have looked forward to it immensely—time to write, rest, pray, and clean, and do all the other errands I have been delaying. But as the day wears on, I find myself longing for my family or friends. I am lonely, and the day isn't even over yet. I would make a terrible hermit.

When I think of a truly prayerful person, I have always imagined a contemplative, someone who spends a lot of time alone. Getting to know God seems like a solitary occupation to me. Prayer involves silence and listening, and that takes alone-time. It seems to me that devoutness is in direct correlation with the ability (and desire) to be comfortable being alone with God. Think of Jesus alone in the desert, Moses alone with God on Mount Sinai, and Elijah hearing the still small voice alone on a mountain. Most visions and revelations happen when someone is alone, so it must be better to be alone. It must be more holy. Or is it?

Scripture is clear from the very beginning that God does not think it is good for us to be alone. When God forms the first human in the story of the Garden of Eden, God observes that human and then states, quite clearly, "It is not good the man should be alone." We were created in the image of God together, not alone. God says that when two or three are gathered, God is in the midst of them.

So why do we assume that the solitary life is the holiest way to find God? Do prayerful people have to spend lots of time alone? Is it the only way to be holy? The only way to find God?

Before Jesus begins his ministry, he deliberately spends time alone in the desert. When he is alone, he is tempted by the devil. After this period of temptation, Jesus returns to minister to people and, though he leaves the crowds to pray alone from time to time, the remainder of his life is spent in the company of others. Jesus's ministry occurs in the presence of people: God manifests the incarnation by sending someone to be with us so that we would not be alone.

I think we should reevaluate our notion that it is better to be alone if we are to be holy. I posit that it's not better (or worse!)—just different. Being alone can be a deepening time with God but so can being in the presence of others. If you are more extroverted and find it hard to be alone for hours on end, you are not more or less holy. You are just different.

We are made in the image of God in the company of others because God is relationship. God in the form of the Trinity is all about companionship and communion and harmony between persons.

Writes John Michael Talbott in *The Lessons of St. Francis*: "It's true: Solitude, silence and stillness help us connect to God. But God doesn't intend that we take such spiritual riches and keep them to ourselves and hoard them away... Intimacy with God becomes a prelude to intimacy with and service to others."

> Measure how much time you spend alone and how much
> time you spend in the company of others. Have you achieved
> a balance that works for you? Which is more life-giving?
> How can you change the way you spend time alone or with
> others to make it more spiritually fulfilling?

The truth about community

The path to well-being lies in right relationship: right relationship between God and humanity and right relationship between people. But it is a tall order to live in the model of the Trinity.

A magic occurs when human beings are united as one. It is a rare phenomenon. These glimpses of harmony when God and humans are in full communion are unpredictable. They can happen during Holy Eucharist or when a preacher connects with listeners. They can happen during a shared moment of profound joy or sadness. They can happen in the office of a counselor when a client has a true insight and the counselor understands, truly understands. Community happens in a dance with the Holy Spirit. It is not predictable. It is not something that can be controlled. But when it happens, it is life changing.

Let me give you an example.

Boys in the Boat is the story of Joe Rantz, a poor kid from Washington state who managed to row crew in the 1936 Olympics. When Joe was on his deathbed at the end of his life, he said the moments he remembered most were when he was rowing with those other young men. He found it hard to articulate what happened in that boat when the boys rowed as one. The book's author, Daniel James Brown, describes it this way:

> There is a thing that sometimes happens in rowing that is hard to achieve and hard to define. Many crews, even winning crews, never really find it. Others find it but can't sustain it. It's called "swing." It only happens when all eight oarsmen are rowing in such perfect unison that no single action by any one is out of sync with those of all the others. It's not just that the oars enter and leave the water at precisely the same instant. Sixteen arms must begin to pull, sixteen knees must begin to fold and unfold, eight bodies must begin to slide forward and backward, eight backs must bend and straighten all at once. Each minute action—each subtle turning of wrists—must be mirrored exactly by each oarsman, from one end of the boat to the other. Only then will the boat continue to run, unchecked, fluidly and gracefully between the pulls of the oars. Only then will it feel as if the boat is part of each of them, moving as if on its own. Only then does pain entirely give way to exultation. Rowing then becomes a kind of perfect language. Poetry, that's what a good swing feels like.

Joe tasted the dynamic relationship between God and people when he and his crewmates achieved "swing." It was harmony between individuals who moved together in such a way as to become one while still maintaining their individuality. When they were in swing, something transcendent emerged. This is what God is like: three in one and one in three. Perfect union among humans and God. A dance beyond any we have ever known.

When a person is dying, they will often recall moments of great love and connection. These moments have been touched by God, and they have an eternal element to them. Memories of them don't fade. These are moments of Trinity.

I believe that the greatest path to God is not an individual path but a path toward one another, a path to community. So long as humanity remains isolated, violent, and lonely, we will not be able to find God. To truly know God, we must learn to love and respect one another. We must discipline ourselves to find connection and to search for moments of harmony and unity, for that is where God is revealed.

But this is hard to do in a world filled with polarities, a world where differences are highlighted and schisms drive the news. Discord, violence, racism, injustice, and controversy attract the attention of the public. We are fascinated with the pain of others, and our appetite is insatiable. Our fascination with our own brokenness and isolation only magnifies the problem, while moments of connection and harmony are rarely noted and rarely shared.

Identify a time in your life when you experienced swing. If you can, share this experience with a small group or individual.

The basic nature of relationship

There is nothing mysterious about this: the world is not divided into stand-alone entities. It is we who divide it into objects for our convenience. A mountain chain is not divided into individual mountains: it is we who divide it up into parts that strike us as in some way separate. A countless number of our definitions, perhaps all of them, are relational: a mother is a mother because she has a child; a planet is a planet because it orbits a star; a predator is such because it hunts prey; a position in space is there only in relation to something else. Even time exists only as a set of relations.

—Carlo Rovelli, *The Order of Time*

According to physicist Carlo Rovelli, relationship is the very fabric of creation. We are known by others and by God and we know ourselves as we relate to others. I am a mother because of my relationship with my sons. I am a priest because of my relationship with my parishioners. I am a writer because you are reading these words. We become who we are by relating to others.

Just as we are known by the way we relate to the world around us, so we learn most from our relationships, particularly the relationships of those closest to us. Love is the greatest catalyst for growth. Our need to love more and better pushes us to redefine our relationships and to become better people.

I have struggled to be a good parent. I have made many mistakes. But being a mom has made me a better person. It has forced me to put others' needs ahead of my own. My relationship with my sons has compelled me to buy foods I don't want—and clean and cook and earn money. I've had to learn how to discipline and then learn how to let go. For all the mistakes I have made, I am clear about one thing: becoming a mother made me grow in ways I never knew I could. And this is true of all relationships that are founded in love.

The most important aspect in a loving relationship is emotional honesty. We must have the courage to tell each other the truth, not in a harsh way but with honesty about what we really need and want. My marriage ended for many reasons, but chief among them was my inability to truly say how I felt. And that is not a mistake I will ever make again. In this new relationship that I am blessed to have found, I am trying very hard to be honest about how I feel, even if the feeling is selfish or silly. For how can another person love me if I don't let them know how I feel?

To be clear, acknowledging a feeling does not mean you need to act upon it or give it more weight than it deserves. If you feel annoyed with someone, you don't have to act upon that feeling. If you feel lazy or sad or angry, it is your responsibility to manage those feelings and not let them take over or lead you to act on impulse. But at the same time, if your loved one asks you how you are feeling, you should tell the truth. They probably already know the answer, or they wouldn't ask. And isn't it refreshing to admit that you can have a feeling, and it is not the end of the world? Feelings don't define us, and they don't have to dictate our behavior. But they should not be ignored. Give them their due: acknowledge their presence, yes, but then move on.

Our feelings, especially in relationship to our loved ones, can tell us a great deal about the lessons that we need to learn. They are messengers, teachers, invitations to learn and grow. But feelings are not our masters. They don't have to be scary, and they don't always have to be alleviated. They just need to be heard.

If relationships are the building blocks of creation, then we must establish relationships that center around our love of God. And this is where the group comes in. We cannot fully understand ourselves as followers of Jesus without a group of fellow disciples to walk with us.

Try communicating a feeling to someone who you love and trust. Practice being truly honest, even if the feeling is embarrassing or negative in some way. Reflect on how this experience assists you in processing and learning.

Forming groups

> For where two or three are gathered in my name,
> I am there among them.
>
> —Matthew 18:20

We cannot come to know God in total isolation. As we have discussed, this is a radical thought, since some of the greatest saints were, in essence, isolated individuals, such as the Desert Fathers or Dame Julian of Norwich, who shut herself in a room attached to the church and lived her entire life alone. But even these solitary souls had people occasionally come to them for prayer or counsel, and they were aware of, and in a sense in relationship with, the world.

The mind is tricky. It is hard to battle the insecurities of the mind without a group of friends. My doctor friend says there is an old saying in medicine: "Never worry alone." We need one another to become the fullness of who we are called to be, to discern God's will and to lead healthy lives.

I love to think of the relationship between Jesus and his mother. In the Gospel of John, they are at a party together. Jesus has long since reached adulthood, and his disciples are with him so he must have begun to teach and preach, but his mom is also at the party. That must have been awkward! When the wine runs out, his mother says these simple words: "They have no wine."

Jesus knows exactly what his mother means with these words because he reacts to her. He asks: "Woman, what have you to do with me?" The translation sounds harsher today than it was meant. Jesus is not being terse, but he is clearly aggravated. His mother is pushing him to perform a miracle, and he is resisting her. But ultimately, his mother prevails, and Jesus does just what she asks. Maybe she gave him that mother-look. Maybe she didn't even have to look. But it was her nudge that brought him into the fullness of his ministry in the Gospel of John. That is the kind of relationship I am talking about—when someone else helps you become who you were meant to be. And just remember: even the Son of God needed a nudge!

Consider then, how much more we desperately need one another. The hardest part of being a parish priest is knowing how profoundly and deeply people could be fed if they took the time to talk to one another. On Sundays, I look out at the pews and see people sitting next to one another: a set of parents whose adult child committed suicide sitting close to another couple whose adult child also died in the same way.

And they don't even know the wounds they share. If only they discovered each other, they could care for and walk aside one another. But they tell me they don't have enough time to meet. What could be more important? What could be more worth the time?

For Practice

Who do you feel you could share your life with? Who may be going through similar circumstances in their life? Who do you trust? Pray about the potential to meet with others and talk about God. And then dare to give it a try. It is a risk, but there are great rewards.

Structure

Once a person experiences a true discipleship group, I have never known a single person to regret joining one. Discipleship groups are that good. But for a small group or discipleship group to truly be a holy relationship— a community—it must have certain specific ingredients.

First, a discipleship group must be confidential. There can be no gossip or sharing of personal information. This boundary must be upheld, or the group will wound itself. Without this very important protection, there can be no truly honest sharing or vulnerability. All must agree and maintain this confidentiality.

Secondly, the group must meet regularly at a set time. And all must attend. It must be a top priority. There cannot be continuity if people do not make this commitment. The time must be protected, stable, and sacred. Everyone in the group needs to be able to count on each other and on the constancy of presence. This is where temptation rears its ugly head once more. Amid the business of life, our minds will play tricks on us and convince us that getting our hair done or making an appointment at the dentist is more important than our group time. We must be strong and trust that this time is sacrosanct. We must make a covenant with the members for the group to be a top priority in our lives, or it will not work. There is no other option.

The group time must center around God. In other words, it cannot be just about sharing your lives. God must be an integral part of the conversation each week. We must agree to support each other in our life with God. What has God called you to do? What is God saying to you? These questions must be addressed.

And finally, there must be fellowship. We need relief, fun, laughter, flexibility, spontaneity. Let each group create its own life-giving practices. Do you knit together? Eat together? Tell a joke? Go bowling once a month? Let the group breathe and simply enjoy each other.

The relationship between these required ingredients is mysterious. Some groups are almost all fun and fellowship but manage to share and to pray. Others are study groups that are almost all academic but check-in with one another and have some fun activities occasionally. And some groups share their lives and then pray for a long time, with a bit of laughter and lots of love. The balance between these is a mystery. Each group finds its way.

I tell my congregation that small groups are like blind dates. Try each other out. You may not be a good fit, and that is okay. Some groups bond for life. Others meet for a season and then disband, and still others are mysteriously like oil and water and simply don't work. All of that is fine. Just let the Spirit move and follow your instincts. And if you find that a group doesn't work out for you, don't give up. Try again, just like you would go on another blind date. You will find your people—or the people that God has chosen to walk with you for a while.

The most effective kind of small group that I have ever experienced is called the discipleship group. It is outlined in detail by Christopher Martin in his book, *The Restoration Project*. He describes a weekly gathering in which disciples of Jesus recite seven vows. These vows are as follows:

> By God's grace, I will set aside time regularly for prayer, "praying to God in secret," working toward twenty minutes a day.

> By God's grace, I will praise God, offering myself and receiving God's love and blessings with the rest of my Christian community in weekly "worship in the beauty of holiness."

By God's grace, I will endeavor to serve others everywhere I can, working toward giving an hour a week in service, remembering that Jesus said, "Surely as you did it to one of the least of these, you did it to me."

By God's grace, I will be a good steward of my money, working toward giving 10 percent to the church and those in need, mindful that "where your treasure is, there your heart will be also."

By God's grace, I will "read, mark, learn, and inwardly digest" the holy Scriptures, trusting that they are "inspired by God" for my "training in righteousness," working toward knowledge of the entire book.

By God's grace, I will do the work God gives me to do this day, remembering that Jesus said, "as the Father has sent me, so I send you," trusting my discipleship group to test and support that call.

By God's grace, we have joined ourselves together as this discipleship group, and we commit to meeting regularly for this season of our lives, believing that "if we love one another, God lives in us, and God's love is perfected in us."

These seven vows anchor the group in the ancient practices of the church, reminding each member that they have a path to walk in, and their group is there to support and nurture them along the journey. The discipleship group is an advanced form of small group, and it is not for everyone.

Many are not yet ready to take these vows, but for those who are ready, there is no greater orientation each week than reciting these simple and powerful words.

Whether you are dipping your toe in a starter small group or ready to try a discipleship group, remember that this practice is near to the heart of Jesus. Our Lord and Savior chose to travel with twelve disciples. He did this intentionally. It was a vital part of his ministry and his own personal support system. He sent them out two by two, and when they returned, they shared the events of the day. This process of sending forth and then gathering was repeated over and over again. Jesus knew that the best kind of spiritual growth and reflection happens when a group of people gather to pray, learn, and reflect together, then they go out into the world to minister and live, only to return and pray and share once more.

For Practice

Gather a group of four or five individuals. Vow to meet once a week for an hour for a limited span of six weeks or so. Follow the instructions from Christopher Martin's book, The Restoration Project. After the six-week period is over, share honestly with one another and see if the group should continue to meet.

Eucharist as gathering

Jesus gathers with his disciples in the Upper Room the night before he dies. The Last Supper is a small-group meeting. It is a dinner among friends.

What would you do if you knew you were going to die the next day? Something tells me that you would gather the people that you love the most. That's what Jesus does. He gathers his group together, and he tells them that he loves them.

The way that Jesus tells his group he loves them is so mystical and magnificent that we have been trying to figure it out ever since. The word that we use to describe this mystery is *eucharist*. It means thanksgiving.

Jesus gathers his disciples, his closest friends. They have given up their lives to follow him, heard his teachings, and traveled from village to village spreading the good news of the kingdom of God. This is his group. These are his people.

What is that mysterious experience that occurs around food? It is like no other kind of group. There is an intimacy involved in eating together, especially in a home. It is as if the act of eating makes us vulnerable to one another. We are acknowledging, in some subconscious way, that we keep one another alive, that we feed one another. We share in the most elemental, essential activity known to humanity, and we nourish our bodies together.

And eating is pleasureful. It is enjoyable. It is an artistic expression, an experience of the senses. No fruit tastes exactly the same, and no meal can be reproduced. Like smell, taste is delicate and intricate. A good meal pleases a person in both body and soul. To share a meal is to be intimate with one another; it is to enjoy life.

For Practice

The next time you gather with people you care about around a dinner table, notice that it is eucharistic. Give thanks either silently or aloud and observe the depth of conversation around the table—the joy, companionship, and even conflict. Notice the potency of this kind of group gathering.

Boundaries

Jesus does not invite everyone to be in his discipleship group. Each member of his group is selected individually by him, and we will never know the exact criteria of the selection process. Some are willing to drop their entire lives and follow him. Other choose different paths, like the young, rich man who is unwilling to give up his wealth and follow Jesus. Many of the people who Jesus healed want to stay with him and follow him, but he sends them away, instructing them not to tell anyone. Why are some invited in, and others sent away?

Jesus is a human being as well as being God. As a human, he models community and intimacy to us. Humans cannot experience community and intimacy without limiting our numbers. The human being can only know so many people intimately and face to face. We must have boundaries and borders to our groups. And here is where things get messy.

We need to understand that boundaries are not the same as prejudice. Groups need limits because we are limited in our capacity to be intimate. We cannot welcome everyone into a small group. We can welcome them to worship, and we can welcome them into baptism and into God's unconditional love, but we cannot welcome everyone into our particular group of disciples. Not even Jesus does that. This is not cruel; it is healthy.

The Episcopal Church welcomes everyone! We are proud and bold to claim this. In a world of racism, homophobia, and other sins, we want to make it clear that God loves all people and wants everyone to come inside the church. But welcoming does not mean that we forgo disciplines, behaviors, and boundaries. Community cannot be a free-for-all, or there would be total chaos. We need guidelines and rules to ensure that safety and kindness abound.

What is the relationship between safety and kindness? Like in so many areas of life, it is a dance. There is a balance between hospitality and discipline. We want to have a healthy community where people are invited into a way of life, and yet we also want to be sure that this way of life is open to all who wish to come.

As you are forming a group, I recommend limiting the size, typically no more than four or five people in the group, if you plan to meet for one hour once a week. Any more than that, and you will not have adequate time to share and to know one another. Any less than that, and you will not experience the breadth of community. Find your sweet spot. And if the group gets too large, make the decision to split in two. I know that this can be heartbreaking, but it is essential that everyone has the time and full attention of the group or God's work cannot be adequately accomplished. Personal gratification or pleasing others must come second to the boundaries of an effective community group setting. Please be firm about this. Have the courage to limit your numbers but do not reject anyone who wants to group with you without giving them another opportunity to meet with others. There should be no rejection, only redirecting into other groups. God wants all of us to gather.

At the same time, certain behaviors cannot be tolerated in a small group, behaviors that risk the well-being of its members. The group must set its own behavioral norms and then adhere to those norms. And if a person does not behave in a manner that is respectful and honoring of others, that person must be asked to leave. This is where Episcopalians tend to fall. We can be so nice that we allow people to sabotage our time. Whole groups will gather and be at the mercy of a dysfunctional person just because no one wants to hurt their feelings or seem unkind. This is itself idolatry. Jesus never said to be nice to everyone; he told us to love them. Sometimes the two are entirely different.

For Practice

Establish boundaries for your group. What are the parameters? What are the agreed upon rules? How can you stay faithful to these rules and who can determine when to say no?

Family

When contemplating a small group, some people will tell me that they have family and don't need or want a church community small group. Family is my community, they say.

Family is different from community. It is not better or worse; it is just different. We have a history with our family members, ties that were forged in the impressionable years of childhood, connections that run deep into our psyches and therefore lack clarity and objectivity. Certainly, God wants us to love and care for our families, as Jesus calls us to love everyone, yet Jesus often calls disciples to leave family behind as they move closer to him. Peter leaves his wife and family, even a sick mother-in-law. The brothers John and James leave their father Zebedee. Even Jesus, when his mother and siblings demand that he come home, claims, "Who is my mother, and who are my brothers?...For whoever does the will of my Father in heaven is my brother and sister and mother" (Matthew 12:48b; 50).

We should love and value our families and spend time with them, but everyone who wants to develop a mature spiritual life must forge relationships not of blood but of faith; we must have what Paul calls brothers and sisters in Christ. These are people who will be honest with us, who see us as we are and not as we should have been or could have been. Our fellow believers are there to support and nurture our journey, not to impose their opinions on us. They do not have the ties and the emotional baggage of family. They are simply on the road with us and together we are trying to follow Jesus.

For Practice

Reflect on Jesus's relationships with his mother and brothers. Give yourself space to love your family but do not expect them to fulfill all your needs.

When a group ends

In the discipleship group vows from Christopher Martin's book, members recite these words: We commit to meeting regularly for this season of our lives.

But what is the right season? And how do we know when the season of our lives comes to an end?

There are a variety of reasons that a group might end. Sometimes a person moves to another state, and the group does not feel that it can meet virtually. Other times, someone dies, and the group simply finds itself at a loss without that the cherished member. There are times when conflict or disagreement severs ties. (As an aside, I find these instances upsetting for it is precisely in our disagreements and disappointments in each other that we can grow the most). Nevertheless, it is okay for a group to come to an end.

If that time has come, it is important to express gratitude to one another and to say farewell. Strive to have a clean and honest departure and don't just neglect each other or fade away. End well and pray for the next group of people that God sends your way.

Your group may also change how it meets. During the pandemic, many groups and classes moved online. Even as circumstances have changed, some groups find they prefer to meet virtually. I have no problem with this. Who am I to deny the presence of the Holy Spirit on a screen? What's important is that the group comes to this decision together, in an honest and frank conversation about the pros and cons of virtual meetings.

I offer another caution for groups that have been meeting for decades. This can be a wonderful experience but take care to ensure that longevity doesn't lead to dysfunction. When a group knows each other for many years, gossip can slide in. It is imperative that each group continues to evaluate itself and to embrace change and diversity.

Lastly, and perhaps more importantly, it's important to remember that there is no perfect group. The exercise of remaining committed to others in the group is part of the spiritual journey. Accepting each other's faults and limitations while continuing to challenge ourselves and others is the dance of love to which God calls us in all our human relationships in this life. No one is perfect. But we can learn so much from one another if we only have the courage to trust each other.

For Practice

If your group is coming to an end, make sure to talk about it and to say thank you. Be very clear as to why and when you will end and help all members to find the support that they need in other group settings.

Finding your group

Let me make this crystal clear: I do not believe it is possible to discern God's will for your life without a group or community to assist you. You simply cannot do this alone. It is impossible. It is like a dog trying to lift itself by pulling on its tail. You don't have the perspective or ability to see yourself clearly; that is simply the state of the human being. We need one another. We were meant to live in relationships with other human beings. Only in these relationships can we reflect the image of God, who is relationship.

ETERNAL GOD, *you made us in your image. Help us to find the other people who make up that group, one that is made in your image and that can discern your will. Help us to never stop seeking our people, the ones with whom you call us to share, to pray, to gather. Our lives will not be complete in you until we have found our fellow disciples. Help us to find our people, Lord. In the name of Jesus who traveled with the twelve. Amen.*

Finding spiritual health

That vision that I had so long ago in my parents' bedroom on Willow Street in New Haven, Connecticut, still sticks with me. What does it mean to love Jesus when the waters of secularism are rising, when technology is changing everything around us? I think it means that we must learn new ways to deepen our relationship with God. We must learn to take care of ourselves spiritually and that means learning the vital signs of the spiritual life so that we can nurture and care for our souls as we would care for our bodies. We must be resilient and strong if we are to learn to breathe underwater!

Find your breath in your time spent with God. Find your pulse in your practices of giving. Find your temperature in the growth that you risk and find your blood pressure in finding your fellow disciples with whom to group. These are the four Gs of the spiritual life, easy to remember but vital to attain and maintain. Pay attention to these vital signs of the spiritual life so that you may learn to breathe and thrive.

I pray that you find this book helpful, that it gives you a fresh perspective. I pray you are filled with joy as you design your spiritual practices and live a life of faith.

Acknowledgments

I have so many people to thank: my new husband, who supports me in ways I never knew possible; my family, Luke, Jake, and Max, my mom and dad, Jonathan and April, and the Carrolls. I am grateful to Barbara, Bob, Christopher, and Chloe, and to my prayer group who have been by my side through so many ups and downs of life. I am truly blessed.

I also want to thank the people of St. John's Cathedral and specifically all those patient souls who listened to this material in lecture form and gave me their honest and sincere feedback.

To Richelle at Forward Movement, whose brilliance in both editing and theological insight continue to astound me.

Most of all, I am grateful to God for the miracle and magnificence of this life.

About the Author

Kate Moorehead Carroll was ordained an Episcopal priest in 1998 in Connecticut. She has spent her entire adult life serving in parishes around the country and currently serves as dean of St. John's Cathedral in Jacksonville, Florida. Kate is married to Chris Carroll, a pediatric intensive care doctor.

Kate produces a podcast called "Find It." FindItwithKate.com

Kate also releases a 4-5-minute morning devotional video on YouTube each morning.

Kate's sermons can be accessed at jaxcathedral.org

About Forward Movement

Forward Movement inspires disciples and empowers evangelists. While we produce great resources like this book, Forward Movement is not a publishing company. We are a discipleship ministry. We live out this ministry through creating and publishing books, daily reflections, studies for small groups, and online resources. People around the world read daily devotions through *Forward Day by Day*, which is also available in Spanish (*Adelante Dia a Dia*) and Braille, online, as a podcast, and as an app for smartphones.

We actively seek partners across the church and look for ways to provide resources that inspire and challenge. A ministry of the Episcopal Church since 1935, Forward Movement is a nonprofit organization funded by sales of resources and gifts from generous donors.

To learn more about Forward Movement and our work, visit us at ForwardMovement.org or VenAdelante.org. We are delighted to be doing this work and invite your prayers and support.